ROONEY

ANNUAL 2008

CONTENTS

WIN A PAIR OF T90s SIGNED BY WAZZA AND COPIES OF FIFA 08

SEE THE WAZZA MENTAL CHALLENGE ON PAGE 49!

If you had asked me at the beginning of the 2006/07 season what I wanted to win most, the FA Cup, European Cup or the Premiership, I would have told you that it had to be the Prem!

For me, it is the most exciting league in the world and to come out on top after 38 hard-fought games makes you the best team in the land!

The last Premiership campaign was easily one of the best yet. While there was the excitement of Chelsea and ourselves going for the main prize, the entire league felt really competitive, with some truly thrilling games and inspired performances.

Players like Dimitar Berbatov, Didier Drogba and, of course, my mate Cristiano Ronaldo put in some amazing performances and there was no shortage of great goals, too. My favourite was when I chipped Portsmouth keeper David James at Old Trafford, while Arsenal's Robin van Persie scored a great goal against Charlton and Paul Scholes scored one of the best volleys ever, against Aston Villa.

And we saw some surprise stars of the season, including Reading's Kevin Doyle, Blackburn's David Bentley and keeper Ben Foster, who's on his way back to Old Trafford after a season at Watford.

Now thoughts turn to the new season, where we start all over again, and after finishing top dog I want to win the Prem even more this time out!

COACH: ARSENE WENGER			
Players	Apps	(Subs)	Goals
Emmanuel Adebayor	21	(8)	8
Jeremie Aliadiere	4	(7)	0
Manuel Almunia	1		0
Gael Clichy	26	(1)	0
Denilson	4	(6)	0
Abou Diaby	9	(3)	1
Johan Djourou	18	(3)	0
Emmanuel Eboue	23	(1)	0
Cesc Fabregas	34	(4)	2
Mathieu Flamini	9	(11)	3
William Gallas	21		3
Thierry Henry	16	(1)	10
Alexander Hleb	27	(6)	2
Justin Hoyte	18	(4)	1
Julio Baptista	11	(13)	3
Jens Lehmann	36		0
Fredrik Ljungberg	16	(2)	0
Mart Poom	1		0
Tomas Rosicky	22	(4)	3
Philippe Senderos	9	(5)	0
Gilberto Silva	34		10
Alexandre Song	1	(1)	0
Kolo Toure	35		3
Robin van Persie	17	(5)	11
Theo Walcott	5	(11)	0

ARSENAL

BARCLAYS PREMIER LEAGUE:	4th
FA CUP:	Fifth Round
CARLING CUP:	Runners-Up
CHAMPIONS LEAGUE:	Second Round
PREMIERSHIP TOP SCORER:	Robin van Persie 11 goals

By Arsene Wenger's own admittance, the 2006-07 season was Arsenal's worst of his 11-year reign in charge. However, it is a reflection of how well Wenger has done that a second successive fourth place finish still represents Arsenal's lowest Premiership position since he took over in 1996.

The Gunners got off to a pants start, failing to win their first three Premiership matches. Ironically, their opening league victory was at Old Trafford when Emmanuel Adebayor scored a wicked late winner. They were to do the 'double' over Manchester United, coming from behind at the Emirates with Thierry Henry scoring a top stoppage time winner. But United would later be happier with the Wenger boys, as their home draw against Chelsea, on May 6, confirmed the Premiership title would be heading back to Old Trafford.

Those two late wins against United belied the underlying fact that Arsenal had failed to finish off too many games throughout the season, particularly in their new Emirates home, and had dropped too many points. As a result, the Gunners never got involved with the title race, with the more pressing concern being to secure a Champions League place again. They had a tussle with Bolton for a while, until a seven-match unbeaten run at the end of the season pulled them safely away from their nearest challengers.

There was some cheer, as a very young Arsenal team lost narrowly to Chelsea in the Carling Cup final. A Theo Walcott goal gave them the lead only for a full-strength Blues side to bounce back with two goals to claim victory.

The bitter taste of defeat was something Arsenal quickly had to get used to as, following the Cardiff disappointment, they were also bundled out of the FA Cup by Blackburn Rovers and the Champions League by PSV Eindhoven.

On a more quirky note, Arsenal scored the most penalties (10) in the Premiership during the season and were involved in the highest scoring game and second biggest win of the season, namely the 6-2 home thrashing of Rovers.

Au revoir Thierry and merci pour les mémoires

PREM FACT ARSENAL TASTED DEFEAT AT THEIR EMIRATES HOME FOR THE FIRST TIME AGAINST WEST HAM, 1-0

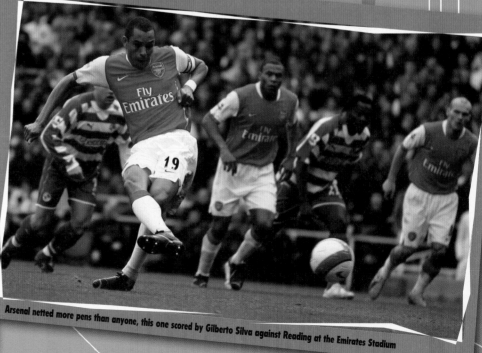

Arsenal netted more pens than anyone, this one scored by Gilberto Silva against Reading at the Emirates Stadium

PREMIERSHIP REVIEW

ASTON VILLA

Barclays Premier League: 11th
FA Cup: Third Round
Carling Cup: Fourth Round
Premiership Top Scorer: Gabriel Agbonlahor 9 goals

Blimey gaffer, you look much bigger on television!

PREM FACT VILLA, ALONG WITH EVERTON, DREW THE MOST AWAY GAMES LAST SEASON - 9

Villa made a wicked start to the Premiership season with a ten-match unbeaten run and finished the season with a nine-match undefeated sequence – earning boss Martin O'Neill the Barclays Manager of the Month award for April.

Unfortunately, these two golden periods, sandwiching a disastrous middle-season run, were never going to be enough to lift Villa out of mid-table mediocrity – a region that has become their natural habitat in recent seasons. On November 11, they beat Everton 1-0, but did not win again in any competition until January 20, when they saw off Watford 2-0. That was 12 games without a win for the Villains and accounted for their drop from the top six and away from a coveted European place. Admittedly they weren't helped by the loss of striker Chris Sutton with a long-term eye injury.

The biggest problem was finishing off games and holding on to leads. Villa managed to draw 17 Premiership matches – more than any other side! If only they could have put away half of those games, Europe would have beckoned.

Villa were dealt a tough hand in both cup competitions after being paired with and losing to Prem champs Manchester United in the FA Cup and Chelsea in the Carling Cup.

Young England star Gabriel Agbonlahor ended up the leading goalscorer with nine goals from his 38 league appearances and Gareth Barry just one behind with eight. Olof Mellberg was one of only a few Premiership players to start every game while former Man United midfielder Eric Djemba-Djemba had one of the shortest ever Premiership seasons: if you blinked you would have missed his sole one-minute substitute appearance! Was it worth it!

Don't worry Nigel, you'll be a Villa player before long!

COACH: MARTIN O'NEILL

Player	Apps	(sub)	Goals
Didier Agathe	0	(5)	0
Gabriel Agbonlahor	37	(1)	9
Juan Pablo Angel	18	(5)	4
Phillip Bardsley	13		0
Milan Baros	10	(7)	1
Gareth Barry	35		8
Patrik Berger	5	(8)	2
Wilfred Bouma	23	(2)	0
Gary Cahill	19	(1)	0
John Carew	11		3
Steven Davis	17	(11)	0
Eric Djemba-Djemba	0	(1)	0
Craig Gardner	11	(2)	2
Lee Hendrie	0	(1)	0
Aaron Hughes	15	(4)	0
Gabor Kiraly	5		0
Martin Laursen	12	(2)	0
Shaun Maloney	5	(3)	1
Gavin McCann	28	(2)	1
Olof Mellberg	38		1
Luke Moore	7	(6)	4
Isaiah Osbourne	6	(5)	0
Stilian Petrov	30		2
Liam Ridgewell	19	(2)	1
Jlloyd Samuel	2	(2)	0
Thomas Sorenson	29		0
Chris Sutton	6	(2)	1
Stuart Taylor	4	(2)	0
Peter Whittingham	2	(1)	0
Ashley Young	11	(2)	2

COACH: MARK HUGHES

Player	Apps	(Sub)	Goals
David Bentley	36		4
Bruno Berner	1		0
Jason Brown	0	(1)	0
Matt Derbyshire	8	(14)	5
David Dunn	7	(4)	0
Brett Emerton	32	(2)	0
Brad Friedel	38		0
Paul Gallagher	2	(14)	1
Michael Gray	10	(1)	0
Stephane Henchoz	10	(2)	2
Francis Jeffers	3	(7)	0
Tugay Kerimoglu	23	(4)	1
Zurab Khizanishvili	17	(1)	0
Shefki Kuqi	0	(1)	0
Benny McCarthy	36		18
James McEveley	3	(1)	0
Aaron Mokoena	18	(9)	0
Lucas Neill	20		0
Ryan Nelson	12		0
Shabani Nonda	17	(9)	7
Andre Ooijer	20		0
Morten Gamst Pedersen	36		6
Sergio Peter	1	(8)	0
Steven Reid	3		0
Jason Roberts	9	(9)	4
Christopher Samba	13	(1)	2
Robbie Savage	21		0
Andy Todd	6	(3)	0
Stephen Warnock	13		1

BLACKBURN ROVERS

Barclays Premier League: 10th
FA Cup: Semi-Final
Carling Cup: Third Round
UEFA Cup: Third Round
Premiership Top Scorer: Benny McCarthy 18 goals

See Michael, this is how you wear your socks

PREM FACT ROVERS GAVE AWAY MORE PENALTIES THAN ANY OTHER PREM SIDE - 11

In Benny McCarthy, a bargain £2.5 million signing from Porto, Blackburn found a deadly marksman who netted 24 goals, including a cool 18 in the Premiership. Mega McCarthy finished behind only Chelsea's Didier Drogba in the Premiership goalscoring stakes, while Rovers also got the best out of former Arsenal midfielder David Bentley, who is now tipped as an England star of the future.

Although McCarthy's goals and Bentley's inspiration boosted Rovers in attack, they were not too hot defensively and had a habit of inflicting damage on themselves. They conceded 11 penalties – more than any other Premiership club – and also had six players sent-off. With the suspensions that followed, it did not give Mark Hughes' side much stability. Boring mid-table mediocrity was, sadly, what they deserved.

What kept the season going was an FA Cup run to the semi-finals. Along the way they booted out Everton, Luton Town, Arsenal and Manchester City before falling to Chelsea in extra-time at Old Trafford. Earlier in the season the Blues had also ended Rovers interest in the Carling Cup.

Blackburn, though, did win a place in the InterToto Cup (a sort of pre-qualifying for the UEFA Cup) after both Portsmouth and Reading could not be bothered to take part.

David Bentley: a future England star?

5

BOLTON WANDERERS

BARCLAYS PREMIER LEAGUE: 7th
FA CUP: Fourth Round
CARLING CUP: Third Round
PREMIERSHIP TOP SCORER: Nicolas Anelka 11 goals

Bolton finished in seventh place in the Premiership and gratefully took the third UEFA Cup spot on the last day of the season, as rivals Reading were held to a 3-3 draw at Blackburn. By then, boss 'Big' Sam Allardyce had announced his departure.

When the season began, it looked as if Bolton were heading for a top four place, and the Champions League beckoned. However, a dreadful loss of form after Christmas, during which time they would win only two further games in the League, soon diminished the club's hopes and ambitions. By February, a 4-1 defeat by Spurs saw the Champions League spot move out of reach.

Not that Bolton made it easy for themselves, picking up a staggering 84 bookings, which was matched only by relegation battlers West Ham United.

In Ricardo Vaz Te, who made 23 appearances from the bench – more than any other Premiership player – they boasted the ultimate 'supersub'. Veteran captain Gary Speed started every match, at the ripe old age of 37, while goalkeeper Jussi Jaaskelainen played every second of the 3420-minute (38-game) Premiership season.

Curiously, without the now departed Jay-Jay Okocha, Wanderers still managed to score more goals (eight) directly from free-kicks than any other side in the top-flight.

PREM FACT GARY SPEED IS THE OLDEST OUTFIELD PLAYER IN THE PREM. HE IS 38-YEARS-OLD THIS SEASON!

COACH: SAM ALLARDYCE

Players	Apps	(Subs)	Goals
Nicolas Anelka	35		11
Tal Ben Haim	30	(2)	0
Ivan Campo	31	(3)	4
Kevin Davies	30		8
El-Hadji Diouf	32	(1)	5
Abdoulaye Faye	29	(3)	2
Quinton Fortune	5	(1)	0
Ricardo Gardner	13	(4)	0
Stelios Giannakopoulos	11	(12)	0
Nicky Hunt	32	(1)	0
Jussi Jaaskelainen	38		0
Cesar Martin	0	(1)	0
Abdoulaye Meite	35		0
Lubomir Michalik	3	(1)	1
Kevin Nolan	31		3
Henrik Pedersen	10	(8)	1
James Sinclair	0	(2)	0
Johann Smith	0	(1)	0
Gary Speed	38		8
Idan Tal	4	(12)	0
Andranik Teymourian	6	(11)	2
David Thompson	3	(5)	0
Ricardo Vaz Te	2	(23)	0

CHARLTON ATHLETIC

BARCLAYS PREMIER LEAGUE: 19th
FA CUP: Third Round
CARLING CUP: Quarter-Final
PREMIERSHIP TOP SCORER: Darren Bent 13 goals

COACH: IAIN DOWIE; LES REED; ALAN PARDEW

Players	Apps	(Subs)	Goals
Darren Ambrose	21	(5)	3
Darren Bent	32		13
Marcus Bent	17	(13)	1
Majid Bougherra	2	(3)	0
Scott Carson	36		0
Souleymane Diawara	18	(5)	0
Talal El Karkouri	36		3
Amady Faye	25	(2)	1
Jonathan Fortune	6	(2)	0
Jimmy Floyd Hasselbaink	11	(14)	2
Matthew Holland	27	(6)	1
Hermann Hreidarsson	30	(1)	0
Bryan Hughes	15	(9)	1
Radostin Kishishev	6	(8)	0
Kevin Lisbie	1	(7)	0
Thomas Myhre	1		0
Omar Pouso	1		0
Darren Randolph	1		0
Andy Reid	15	(1)	2
Dennis Rommedahl	19	(9)	0
Lloyd Sam	3	(4)	0
Osei Sankofa	9		0
Alexandre Song Bilong	12		0
Gonzalo Sorondo	0	(1)	0
Ben Thatcher	10	(1)	0
Jerome Thomas	16	(4)	3
Djimi Traore	11		0
Luke Young	29		1
Zhi Zheng	8	(4)	1

It was a wretched season for Charlton, which saw three different managers in charge, knocked out of the two domestic trophies by lower league opposition (Nottingham Forest and Wycombe Wanderers) and, ultimately, relegation.

Alan Curbishley had ended his 15-year reign at the club the previous season, in which time he had made Charlton a permanent fixture in the Premiership. In fact, over the previous six seasons the side had hovered comfortably between seventh and 14th place – making a mockery of the fans who booed him in his final months at the club.

His successor, Iain Dowie, lasted just 12 games and became the first Prem manager of the season to be sacked. Charlton were in the relegation zone and their future looked bleak. Too dependent on Darren Bent to score the goals, he alone could not outstrip what they were routinely conceding at the back.

Les Reed took charge for eight games with no material improvement, leaving the post by 'mutual consent'. Alan Pardew, sacked by West Ham two weeks earlier, was then drafted in at Christmas then with six games remaining, the Addicks managed to elevate themselves to 17th place. However, it proved false hope and on May 7, a 2-0 defeat by London rivals Tottenham at The Valley confirmed Charlton's demotion from the Premiership.

It says much that a side who conceded 60 goals in the league had as their Player of the Year Scott Carson, who had spent the season on loan from Liverpool.

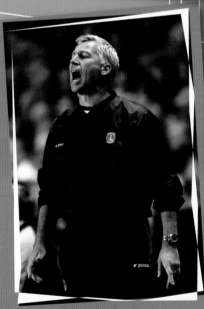

Alan Pardew couldn't stop the rot

PREM FACT SIX YEARS IN THE PREMIERSHIP COMES TO AN END FOR THE ADDICKS

Addicks fans gear themselves up for a trip to Scunthorpe!

CHELSEA

COACH: JOSE MOURINHO

Players	Apps	(Subs)	Goals
Michael Ballack	23	(3)	4
Khalid Boulahrouz	10	(3)	0
Wayne Bridge	17	(5)	0
Ricardo Carvalho	31		3
Petr Cech	20		0
Ashley Cole	21	(2)	0
Joe Cole	3	(10)	0
Carlo Cudicini	7	(1)	0
Lassana Diarra	7	(3)	0
Didier Drogba	32	(4)	20
Michael Essien	33		2
Paulo Ferreira	18	(6)	0
Geremi	15	(4)	1
Henrique Hilario	11		0
Sam Hutchinson	0	(1)	0
Salomon Kalou	19	(14)	7
Frank Lampard	36	(1)	11
Claude Makelele	26	(3)	1
John Obi Mikel	10	(12)	0
Nuno Morais	0	(2)	0
Arjen Robben	16	(5)	2
Ben Sahar	0	(3)	0
Andrei Shevchenko	22	(8)	4
Scott Sinclair	1	(1)	0
John Terry	27	(1)	1
Shaun Wright-Phillips	13	(14)	2

Moneybags Chelsea did the Carling Cup and FA Cup 'double' by beating Arsenal 2-1 in an entertaining final at Cardiff's Millennium Stadium, and then overcoming Manchester United 1-0 after extra-time at the new Wembley in what was a truly dull FA Cup final. The goalscoring hero of both games was dynamite Didier Drogba, who had a sensational season scoring 33 goals in all competitions, while topping the Premiership goal charts with 20 goals. While Drogba was runner-up in the PFA Player of the Year Award, the Ivorian was voted African Player of the Year.

In Europe, Chelsea were heartbroken when they came within a whisker of appearing in their first Champions League final, losing to Liverpool in a second-leg penalty shoot-out (4-1) at Anfield, after the scores were tied at 1-1 on aggregate.

Looking to hold on to the title they had won for the past two seasons, the Premiership title race was all about Chelsea and Manchester United. Unfortunately, the Blues were always the chasing side and, disappointingly, couldn't take their chances to overtake or close the gap when United did slip up. The decisive match day was April 28 when Chelsea squandered a lead and were held to a 2-2 draw by Bolton, just as the Red Devils overcame a 2-0 deficit beating Everton 4-2 at Goodison Park. A useless Chelsea draw with Arsenal in their next game saw the Premiership trophy leave for Old Trafford.

Don't celebrate too soon lads!

Chelsea's cause was not helped when goalkeeper Petr Cech suffering a fractured skull in a collision with Reading's Stephen Hunt, and his replacement Carlo Cudicini was also hurt in the same match. Joe Cole and John Terry were out for a period too but the Blues still boasted the best defence in the Premiership conceding just 24 goals.

The biggest loser of the season was Andrei Shevchenko, a £30 million signing that failed to impress Jose Mourinho, the Chelsea fans or the Premiership, despite being favoured by owner Roman Abramovich.

The Abramovich/Mourinho relationship was the source of much speculation, but after another two trophies in the cabinet it would be a hard and very unpopular move by the Stamford Bridge owner to sack The Special One.

Under Mourinho's reign, Chelsea have gone a staggering record 57 home games without defeat. If their form is maintained, Blues will continue to challenge for honours, including the Holy Grail of the Champions League.

PREM FACT CHELSEA HAVE GONE 57 GAMES UNDEFEATED AT STAMFORD BRIDGE

I am the Special One so give me back my Prem title right now!

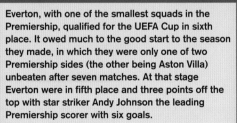

EVERTON

Everton, with one of the smallest squads in the Premiership, qualified for the UEFA Cup in sixth place. It owed much to the good start to the season they made, in which they were only one of two Premiership sides (the other being Aston Villa) unbeaten after seven matches. At that stage Everton were in fifth place and three points off the top with star striker Andy Johnson the leading Premiership scorer with six goals.

Everton always stayed in touch with the European places throughout the season although technically their place was not secure until the final day following a 1-1 draw with Chelsea.

The fact was, with impressive signings Johnson, who ended up with 11 Premiership goals for the season, and Joleon Lescott, along with the wicked Mikel Arteta, who was one of the most fouled players in the Premiership, Everton could and should have done better. They drew 13 matches that easily could have been transferred into some wins.

Joseph Yobo earned the distinction of being the only outfield player in the Premiership who played every minute of all 38 Premiership games. On loan goalkeeper Tim Howard would have played very minute too, but was forced to sit out the two matches against his club Manchester United.

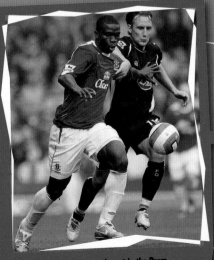

Yobo never had a moment's rest in the Prem

PREM FACT JOSEPH YOBO WAS THE PREM'S ONLY OUTFIELD PLAYER TO PLAY EVERY MINUTE OF ALL 38 PREM GAMES

COACH: DAVID MOYES

Players	Apps	(Subs)	Goals
De Frenca Anderson	0	(1)	0
Victor Anichebe	5	(14)	3
Mikel Arteta	35		9
James Beattie	15	(18)	2
Tim Cahill	17	(1)	5
Lee Carsley	38		1
Simon Davies	13	(2)	1
Manuel Fernandes	8	(1)	2
Tony Hibbert	12	(1)	0
Tim Howard	36		0
Mark Hughes	0	(1)	0
Andy Johnson	32		11
Kevin Kilbane	2		0
Joleon Lescott	36	(2)	2
James McFadden	6	(13)	2
Gary Naysmith	10	(5)	0
Phil Neville	35		0
Nuno Valente	10	(4)	0
Leon Osman	31	(3)	3
Alan Stubbs	23		2
Iain Turner	1		0
Andy van der Meyde	5	(3)	0
James Vaughan	7	(7)	4
David Weir	2	(3)	0
Richard Wright	1		0
Joseph Yobo	38		2

FULHAM

BARCLAYS PREMIER LEAGUE: 16th

FA CUP: Fifth Round

CARLING CUP: Second Round

PREMIERSHIP TOP SCORER: Brian McBride 9 goals

American signing Clint Dempsey gets the better of Liverpool's Xavi Alonso during the 1-0 win at Craven Cottage in May

Clint Dempsey, a £2million signing from American MLS side New England Revolution in January, scored the goal that virtually assured Fulham of their Premiership place. It was netted in the penultimate match of the season, a 1-0 home win over Liverpool on May 5. Two days later relegation rivals Charlton Athletic lost 2-0 to Tottenham and safety was assured.

Three games earlier, the Northern Ireland boss Lawrie Sanchez succeeded Chris Coleman, who had been dismissed following a 15-game run in which Fulham won only once. Sanchez inherited a side that was just four points above the relegation zone and he immediately set a seven-point target from the last five games to ensure survival.

Defensively, Fulham were poor, conceding 60 goals (the same as relegated Charlton) but they also drew an awful lot of games. Indeed, over Christmas and New Year, the west Londoners drew six successive matches – they must have got pencils as Xmas presents – and the points dropped coincided with a fall in their league position.

One happy record was achieved on the last day of the season when Sanchez gave a debut to Matthew Briggs who, at 16 years and 65 days old, became the youngest player ever to play in the Premiership.

COACH: CHRIS COLEMAN; LAWRIE SANCHEZ

Players	Apps	(Subs)	Goals
Luis Boa Morte	12	(3)	0
Carlos Bocanegra	25	(4)	5
Matthew Briggs	0	(1)	0
Michael Brown	33		0
Jimmy Bullard	4		2
Philippe Christanval	19	(1)	1
Simon Davies	14		2
Clint Dempsey	1	(9)	1
Papa Bouba Diop	19	(3)	0
Heidar Helguson	15	(13)	3
Claus Jensen	10	(2)	2
Collins John	8	(14)	1
Zat Knight	21	(1)	2
Jan Lastuvka	7	(1)	0
Brian McBride	34	(3)	9
Vincenzo Montella	3	(7)	2
Antti Niemi	30		0
Ian Pearce	21		1
Franck Queudrue	27	(1)	0
Tomasz Radzinski	25	(9)	2
Liam Rosenior	38		0
Wayne Routledge	13	(10)	0
Bjorn Runstrom	0	(1)	0
Alexei Smertin	5		0
Moritz Volz	23	(5)	2

LIVERPOOL

BARCLAYS PREMIER LEAGUE: Third Place

FA CUP: Third Round

CARLING CUP: Quarter-Final

CHAMPIONS LEAGUE: Runners-Up

PREMIERSHIP TOP SCORER: Dirk Kuyt 12 goals

COACH: RAFAEL BENITEZ

Players	Apps	(Subs)	Goals
Daniel Agger	23	(4)	2
Xabi Alonso	29	(3)	4
Alvaro Arbeloa	8	(1)	1
Fabio Aurelio	10	(7)	0
Craig Bellamy	23	(4)	7
Jamie Carragher	34	(1)	1
Peter Crouch	19	(13)	9
Jerzy Dudek	2		0
Nabil El Zahr	0	(3)	0
Steve Finnan	32	(1)	0
Robbie Fowler	6	(10)	3
Steven Gerrard	35	(1)	7
Mark Gonzalez	14	(11)	2
Danny Guthrie	0	(3)	0
Sami Hyppia	23		2
Emiliano Insua	2		0
Harry Kewell	0	(2)	1
Jan Kromkamp	1		0
Dirk Kuyt	27	(7)	12
Luis Garcia	11	(6)	3
Javier Mascherano	7		0
Daniele Padelli	1		0
Gabriel Paletta	2	(1)	0
Jermaine Pennant	20	(14)	1
Jose Reina	35		0
John Arne Riise	29	(4)	1
Mohamed Sissoko	15	(1)	0
Stephen Warnock	1	0	
Boudewijn Zenden	9	(7)	0

Liverpool reached the Champions League final for the second time in three years, having began their quest in the third qualifying round before the Premiership season had even kicked off! Along the way they accounted for some notable scalps, including Bordeaux, Galatasaray, Barcelona, PSV Eindhoven and Chelsea before losing to AC Milan 2-1 in the final in Athens, Greece.

At home, the season began well when they beat Chelsea 2-1 in the Community Shield in Cardiff, but the race for the Premiership title eluded them as Manchester United and Chelsea soon pulled away. Still, the Reds managed to earn Champions League qualification for 2007-08 long before the season's end, then edged out Arsenal for third place on goal difference. This was thanks to the injury-recovered Harry Kewell's dramatic stoppage time equaliser against Charlton on the last day of the season at Anfield.

In the two domestic cup competitions they were undone at Anfield by Arsenal on both occasions. A third round exit in the FA Cup was followed by a quarter-final loss in the Carling Cup. In a breathtaking game, the Reds were on the wrong end of a ghastly 6-3 scoreline by a young Gunners side.

Ace striker Peter Crouch was one of only three players to score a hat-trick in the Premiership when he netted three times in a 4-1 home win over... Arsenal!

Liverpool were also disciplined and strong. They were the only Premiership side not to have a player sent-off and they gave away just one penalty in the League. Jose Reina achieved more clean sheets than any other goalkeeper, stopping the opposition from scoring on 18 occasions.

There was some silverware when Liverpool's youngsters lifted the FA Youth Cup, beating Manchester United in a penalty shoot-out. The future, therefore, looks in good hands.

PREM FACT LIVERPOOL WERE THE ONLY PREMIERSHIP SIDE NOT TO HAVE A PLAYER SENT-OFF

Pirlo goes for goal as AC Milan beat Liverpool in the Champions League final in Athens

MANCHESTER CITY

Barclays Premier League: 14th ★★★
FA Cup: Quarter-Final
Carling Cup: Second Round
Premiership Top Scorer: Joey Barton 6 goals

Coach: Stuart Pearce			
Players	Apps	(Subs)	Goals
Michael Ball	12		0
Joey Barton	32		6
DeMarcus Beasley	10	(7)	3
Bernardo Corradi	19	(5)	3
Ousmane Dabo	10	(3)	0
Paul Dickov	8	(7)	0
Sylvain Distin	36		2
Richard Dunn	38		1
Dietmar Hamann	12	(4)	0
Joe Hart	1		0
Stephen Ireland	14	(10)	1
Andreas Isaksson	12	(2)	0
Sun Jihai	10	(3)	0
Michael Johnson	10		0
Stephen Jordan	12	(1)	0
Ishmael Miller	3	(13)	0
Danny Mills	0	(1)	0
Matthew Mills	1		0
Emile Mpenza	9	(1)	3
Nedum Onouha	15	(3)	0
Claudio Reyna	11	(3)	0
Micah Richards	27		1
Gerogios Samaras	15	(19)	4
Trevor Sinclair	13	(4)	0
Daniel Sturridge	0	(2)	0
Ben Thatcher	10		0
Hatem Trabelsi	16	(3)	1
Darius Vassell	28	(3)	3
Nicky Weaver	24		0

It was a truly pants season to be a Manchester City fan. Arch-rivals United were back to trophy-winning ways while the blue half of the city continued with their interminable soap-like story of inept club management. No-one has ever said that it's fun being a Manchester City fan!

City always struggled to score. At home they managed a mere ten goals in the Premiership and only 29 overall (only bottom club Watford equalled it). In all, City fans, if they went to every one of their club's league matches, only got to see 73 goals, for and against – less than any other Premiership club contrived, and not a great recipe for entertainment. No wonder City fans are considered to have the best sense of humour in the entire Premiership!

Forward Georgios Samaras was a massive disappointment managing a pitiful four goals – the last of which was on New Year's Day – in 34 appearances.

Ill-discipline also plagued the side. Ever-controversial Joey Barton, although the team's top scorer with six goals, was involved in a major bust-up with team-mate Ousmane Dabo during training and was suspended by the club for the last two games of the season. Unsurprisingly, he departed for new pastures shortly after. Michael Ball did himself no favours either when he deliberately stamped on Ronaldo in the first minute of the Manchester derby in May.

The season ended with the dismissal of manager Stuart Pearce (pictured, top right) – but their is now light at the end of the tunnel after Sven Goran-Eriksson became the club's 20th boss since Alex Ferguson took over at Old Trafford.

Captain Richard Dunne was voted City's Player of the Season for the third successive year while Micah Richards was voted the club's Young Player of the Season for the second successive time.

City's Richard Dunne gets the better of United's Alan Smith

PREM FACT CITY SCORED A PALTRY TEN GOALS AT EASTLANDS IN THE PREM LAST SEASON!

PREM FACT VIDUKA AND YAKUBA SCORED OVER 60% OF MIDDLESBROUGH'S GOALS WITH 26 BETWEEN THEM

MIDDLESBROUGH

Barclays Premier League: 12th
FA Cup: Quarter-Final
Carling Cup: Second Round
Premiership Top Scorer: Mark Viduka 14 goals

Coach: Gareth Southgate			
Players	Apps	(Subs)	Goals
Julio Arca	18	(3)	2
George Boateng	34		1
Lee Cattermole	21	(9)	1
Malcolm Christie	4	(9)	1
Andrew Davies	21	(2)	0
Stewart Downing	33		2
Jason Euell	8	(8)	0
Danny Graham	0	(1)	0
Robert Huth	7	(4)	1
Adam Johnson	3	(9)	0
Brad Jones	2		0
Dong Gook Lee	3	(6)	0
Massimo Maccarone	1	(5)	1
Gaizka Mendieta	4	(3)	0
James Morrison	15	(12)	2
Stuart Parnaby	8	(9)	0
Emanuel Pogatetz	34		2
Chris Riggott	5	(1)	0
Fabio Rochemback	16	(3)	2
Mark Schwarzer	35		0
Andrew Taylor	34		0
Mark Viduka	22	(7)	14
David Wheater	1	(1)	1
Johnathan Woodgate	29		0
Abel Xavier	14		1
Aiyegbeni Yakubu	35	(1)	12

Middlesbrough, under rookie boss Gareth Southgate, finished the season two positions higher than they had the previous year under England boss Steve McClaren. Some of Middlesbrough's performances were impressive and they enjoyed a good run in the FA Cup reaching the quarter-finals where they lost out to Manchester United after forcing a replay at Old Trafford.

If there was a thorn in Middlesbrough's side it was United's Portuguese star Ronaldo who won (sometimes controversially) and converted three penalties against them in three separate matches – including that FA Cup replay.

Repacing Southgate as central defender, local lad and prodigal son Jonathan Woodgate arrived on loan from Real Madrid. Such was the ease with which he adapted back to life in the Premiership that in April Boro announced that they had signed him on a permanent deal for £7m.

The second-half of the season saw the re-emergence of the unstoppable Aussie striker Mark Viduka, following a lay-off from injury. In his last 22 League and cup games Viduka found the net a crucial 16 times, including a brace on the final day in a 3-1 win against Fulham, and in so doing made certain Middlesbrough would finish above Newcastle in the table – making them the top dogs in the North-East. The Toon were suitably impressed, signing 'Viduks' this summer.

Gaffer Southgate adopted that stylish geography teacher look

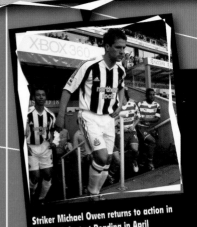

Striker Michael Owen returns to action in the 1-0 defeat at Reading in April

NEWCASTLE UNITED

BARCLAYS PREMIER LEAGUE: 13th
FA CUP: Third Round
CARLING CUP: Quarter-Final
UEFA CUP: Round of 16
PREMIERSHIP TOP SCORER: Obafami Martins 11 goals

Glenn Roeder finally resigned as Newcastle United manager following a 2-0 home defeat by Blackburn in the penultimate game of the season. It was the fifth successive game in which the Toon had failed to score and extended a totally goalless run at home that went all the way back to February 10 (when they had put two past Liverpool at St James' Park). It was Newcastle's worst goalless home run in 56 years and to add insult to injury they won just one of Roeder's last ten games in charge.

All in all it was a grey season for the black and white army, who witnessed early exits in the FA Cup (a 5-1 home defeat by Championship side Birmingham) and UEFA Cup (to AZ Alkmaar). Injuries to key players such as Shola Ameobi and Shay Given, coupled with the long-term absence of hugely missed Michael Owen contributed to the Magpies' poor form.

Owen finally returned to action on April 30 at Reading, the first time that he had played a full 90 minutes since Boxing Day 2005. He came through with flying colours and now big things are expected of him this season.

To lift some of the gloom that's descended on the Tyne, Sam Allardyce was installed as Newcastle's fourth manager in three years this summer and he quickly went about buying Joey Barton from Manchester City and Australian striker Mark Viduka from Middlesbrough.

Shortly after it was also announced billionaire businessman Mike Ashley was on the verge of buying the club.

COACH: GLENN ROEDER

Players	Apps	(Subs)	Goals
Shola Ameobi	9	(3)	3
Celestine Babayaro	12		0
Titus Bramble	17		0
Nicky Butt	27	(4)	1
Stephen Carr	23		0
Andrew Carroll	0	(4)	0
Damien Duff	20	(2)	1
Kieron Dyer	20	(2)	5
David Edgar	2	(1)	1
Belozoglu Emre	21	(3)	2
Shay Given	22		0
Steve Harper	15	(3)	0
Paul Huntington	10	(1)	1
Albert Luque	0	(7)	0
Obafemi Martins	32	(1)	11
James Milner	31	(4)	3
Craig Moore	17		0
Charles N'Zogbia	10	(12)	0
Alan O'Brien	1	(1)	0
Oguchi Onyewu	7	(4)	0
Michael Owen	3		0
Scott Parker	28	(1)	3
Matthew Pattison	2	(5)	0
Peter Ramage	20	(1)	0
Giuseppe Rossi	3	(8)	0
Antoine Sibierski	14	(12)	3
Nolberto Solano	25	(3)	0
Pavel Srnicek	1	(1)	0
Steven Taylor	26	(1)	2

PORTSMOUTH

BARCLAYS PREMIER LEAGUE: 9th
FA CUP: Fourth Round
CARLING CUP: Third Round
PREMIERSHIP TOP SCORER: Nwankwo Kanu 10 goals

"I'm not entirely sure this Brylcreem sponsorship deal is going to work out for me!"

Portsmouth showed the best improvement of any side in the Premiership, finishing eight places higher than they did in 2005-06. Indeed, ninth place was their best finishing position in 50 years. It might have been even better if a controversial refereeing decision had gone their way when, on the last day of the season against Arsenal, lino Darren Cain informed ref Graham Poll that he thought Niko Kranjcar's winning goal was offside and should be disallowed. Television pictures suggested it might well have been legitimately scored and the three points would have put Portsmouth into the UEFA Cup.

Portsmouth's Player of the Season was goalkeeper David James – and deservedly so. James established a new clean sheets record for the top-flight, keeping 143 of them. The record-breaking feat was achieved in the goalless draw with Arsenal on the last day of the season, during which he saved a penalty from Julio Baptista.

James – who played in every minute of every game – along with the club's back-four, were chiefly responsible for Portsmouth's great start. They did not concede a goal in the first four games, while later in the season James almost set another new record for the most successive sequence of clean sheets – only to be cruelly denied by John O'Shea's stoppage-time consolation for Manchester United in a 2-1 win for Pompey. Much is now expected of Harry Redknapp's men as they push for a Uefa Cup spot.

Mutual respect: Wayne's audacious chip over the Portsmouth keeper prompts a smile on both players' faces

COACH: HARRY REDKNAPP

Players	Apps	(Subs)	Goals
	32		1
Sol Campbell	5	(13)	3
Andy Cole	29	(2)	0
Sean Davis	1	(4)	
Rodolph Douala	7	(3)	
Manuel Fernandes	11	(7)	
Richard Hughes	38		
David James	25	(1)	
Glen Johnson	32	(4)	10
Nwankwo Kanu	0	(1)	
Ognjen Koroman	11	(13)	2
Niko Kranjcar	9	(1)	0
Lauren	8	(14)	2
Lomana Tresor LuaLua	1	(6)	1
Arnold Mvuemba	25	(6)	6
Benjani Mwaruwari	1	(2)	0
Andrew O'Brien	35		1
Gary O'Neil	21	(2)	2
Noe Pamarot	25	(1)	2
Pedro Mendes	36		2
Linvoy Primus	20		0
Dejan Stefanovic	30	(5)	8
Matthew Taylor	5	(7)	0
David Thompson	1	(3)	2
Svetoslav Todorov	10		0
Djimi Traore			

READING

Barclays Premier League: 8th

FA Cup: Fourth Round

Carling Cup: Third Round

Premiership Top Scorer: Kevin Doyle 13 goals

In their first ever season in the top-flight, Steve Coppell's Reading turned out to be a breath of fresh air. They played in a number of totally thrilling league and cup games, quite happy to score and concede – which made for wonderful entertainment value along the way.

The Royals also came within a point of qualifying for the UEFA Cup. On the last day of the season they played a see-saw of a match against Blackburn in which they led twice, but the game ended 3-3 and with it the prospect of European football at the Madjeski Stadium… for now.

In the FA Cup they came mighty close to staging the most unlikely comeback of the season; having trailed 3-0 to Manchester United after six minutes at the Mad Stad, they managed to claw their way back to 3-2. After hitting the crossbar in stoppage time, Coppell's boys were gutted not to earn the draw they so richly deserved. Similarly, in the Carling Cup, they were on the wrong end of a seven-goal thriller against Liverpool – losing 4-3 at Anfield.

In Kevin Doyle Reading found a cool striker until injury sidelined him, while in Nicky Shorey they have a brilliant left-back who was called up for the senior national side against Brazil – the first Reading player to represent England. Ivar Ingimarsson was deservedly the club's Player of the Year for his stalwart performances in front of goalkeeper Marcus Hahnemann. Both players were ever-present, while Shorey missed just one match.

One of the highlights of Reading's first season in the Premiership was the 6-0 thrashing of West Ham – the biggest win of the season for any club. The only downside of a remarkable year was the inevitable attention of bigger clubs and Steve Sidwell, Reading's feisty midfielder, packed his bags to join Chelsea on a free transfer.

Prem Fact READING WON PROMOTION TO THE TOP-FLIGHT ON MARCH 25, 2006 WHICH WAS EARLIER IN THE SEASON THAN ANY OTHER POST-WAR SIDE

Coach: Steve Coppell

Players	Apps	(Subs)	Goals
Andre Bikey	7	(8)	0
Bobby Convey	9	(1)	0
Ulises De la Cruz	9		1
Kevin Doyle	28	(4)	13
Michael Duberry	8		0
Adam Federici	0	(2)	0
Brynjar Gunnarsson	10	(13)	3
Marcus Hahnemann	38		0
Greg Halford	2	(1)	0
James Harper	36	(2)	3
Stephen Hunt	28	(7)	4
Ivar Ingimarsson	38		2
Seol Ki-hyeon	22	(5)	4
Dave Kitson	9	(4)	2
Leroy Lita	22	(11)	7
Glen Little	18	(6)	0
Shane Long	9	(12)	2
Graeme Murty	23		0
John Oster	6	(19)	1
Nicky Shorey	37		1
Steve Sidwell	35		4
Sam Sodje	2	(1)	0
Ibrahima Sonko	23		1

The Royals will miss the tenacious Steve Sidwell in midfield

Leroy Lita scores the fifth of six goals as Royals hammer West Ham on New Year's Day

SHEFFIELD UNITED

Barclays Premier League: 18th

FA Cup: Third Round

Carling Cup: Third Round

Premiership Top Scorer: Rob Hulse 8 goals

New arrivals in the Premiership, Blades spent almost the entire season hovering above the relegation zone. But on the last day of the season they were beaten at home 2-1 by fellow-relegation battlers Wigan (with superb irony it was Sheffield United old boy David Unsworth who scored the winning penalty in the 45th minute), and West Ham won away at champions Manchester United. It meant that Wigan and United both ended up on 38 points and the Blades would suffer the pain of relegation by the cruelest of margins – a goal difference of 1! Some calculated the cost of that solitary goal to be worth a mega £40 million.

The Hammers' win at Old Trafford was particularly galling. The FA Premier League had 'merely' fined West Ham £5 million for irregularities related to the acquisition and registration of Argentinean World Cup star Carlos (Apache) Tevez. Wigan, Charlton, Fulham and now relegated Sheffield United firmly believed that West Ham should have been docked points in addition to the fine, a punishment that would have massively altered the outcome of the season. It's an issue that rumbles on. Of course it was Tevez's strike that gave West Ham their victory in Manchester.

The defeat by Wigan was United's 20th of the season and in the end it proved too much for boss Neil Warnock who failed to agree new terms and resigned after seven years in charge.

United had looked set to be mid-table material but their inconsistency – winning one and then losing or drawing the next two or three games – proved their undoing.

In the FA Cup they were also embarrassed by League One outfit Swansea City at home and in the Carling Cup it was the same story with Championship side Birmingham City.

Blades fan and actor Sean Bean adds his weight to the Yorkshire club's ultimately unsuccessful bid to stay in the top-flight

Coach: Neil Warnock

Players	Apps	(Subs)	Goals
Ade Akinbiyi	2	(1)	0
Chris Armstrong	24	(3)	0
Ian Bennett	2		0
Leigh Bromby	12	(5)	0
Claude Davis	18	(3)	0
Ahmed Fathi	2	(1)	0
Derek Geary	26		0
Paul Gerrard	2		0
Keith Gillespie	27	(4)	2
Rob Hulse	28	(1)	8
Paul Ifill	3		0
Phil Jagielka	38		4
Steven Kabba	0	(7)	0
Colin Kazim-Richards	15	(12)	1
Patrick Kenny	34		0
Matthew Kilgarron	6		0
Robert Kozluk	17	(2)	0
Nicholas Law	2	(2)	0
Mikele Leigertwood	16	(3)	0
Chris Lucketti	8		0
Nick Montgomery	22	(4)	0
Chris Morgan	21	(3)	1
Christian Nade	7	(18)	3
Alan Quinn	15		2
Stephen Quinn	11	(8)	0
Luton Shelton	2	(2)	0
David Sommell	4	(1)	0
Jonathan Stead	12	(2)	5
Michael Tonge	23	(4)	2
David Unsworth	5		0
Danny Webber	13	(9)	3
Alan Wright	1		0

Prem Fact ROB HULSE SCORED THE FIRST GOAL OF THE 2006-07 SEASON AGAINST LIVERPOOL ON AUGUST 19, 2006

TOTTENHAM HOTSPUR

BARCLAYS PREMIER LEAGUE: 5th

FA Cup: Quarter-Final

CARLING Cup: Semi-Final

UEFA Cup: Quarter-Final

PREMIERSHIP TOP SCORER: Dimitar Berbatov 12 goals

In Dimitar Berbatov, a more-than-earned-his-keep £10.8 million signing from Bayer Leverkusen, Tottenham bought a human goal machine. The 26-year-old Bulgarian was cool enough to score Tottenham's first and last goals of a 59-game season that saw the London club reach the last eight of the FA Cup and UEFA Cup, and the semi-finals of the Carling Cup. The Tottenham Player of the Year ended his first campaign in England with a haul of 23 goals in all competitions.

Tottenham were arguably the Premiership's most entertaining side. In all, there were 111 goals scored for and against Spurs and they finished with a +3 goal difference. Certainly, the goals-against column was influenced by the injury to skipper Ledley King, but fellow centre-half Michael Dawson impressed, playing in all but one of Tottenham's League, cup and European matches, while goalkeeper Paul Robinson was an ever-present in the Premiership.

Across all competitions, Spurs fans celebrated over 100 goals with the century inevitably scored by Berbatov, against Charlton in a 2-0 win that relegated their opponents.

Another crack at the UEFA Cup was secured with games to spare as Tottenham matched their previous season's fifth-placed finish. The only negative was that they finished behind arch-rivals Arsenal once again – this time by six points.

Berbatov became one of the finds of last season, with a host of bigger clubs trying to sign him in the summer

Robbie Keane nets after two minutes in Seville. It was to no avail as the Spaniards went on to win 4-3 on aggregate. Note worst away shirts of any Prem team – yes, they are brown!

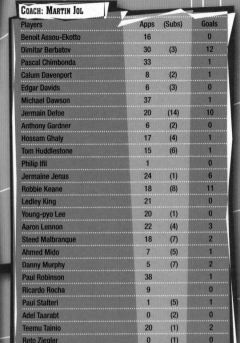

COACH: MARTIN JOL

Players	Apps	(Subs)	Goals
Benoit Assou-Ekotto	16		0
Dimitar Berbatov	30	(3)	12
Pascal Chimbonda	33		1
Calum Davenport	8	(2)	1
Edgar Davids	6	(3)	0
Michael Dawson	37		1
Jermain Defoe	20	(14)	10
Anthony Gardner	6	(2)	0
Hossam Ghaly	17	(4)	1
Tom Huddlestone	15	(6)	1
Philip Ifil	1		0
Jermaine Jenas	24	(1)	6
Robbie Keane	18	(8)	11
Ledley King	21		0
Young-pyo Lee	20	(1)	0
Aaron Lennon	22	(4)	3
Steed Malbranque	18	(7)	2
Ahmed Mido	7	(5)	1
Danny Murphy	5	(7)	2
Paul Robinson	38		1
Ricardo Rocha	9		0
Paul Stalteri	1	(5)	1
Adel Taarabt	0	(2)	0
Teemu Tainio	20	(1)	2
Reto Ziegler	0	(1)	0
Didier Zokora	26	(5)	0

WATFORD

BARCLAYS PREMIER LEAGUE: 20th

FA Cup: Semi-Final

CARLING Cup: Fourth Round

PREMIERSHIP TOP SCORER: Hameur Bouzza 5 goals

There was something painfully predictable about the way Watford's season would unfold in their brief return to the Premiership. From the off they were seriously out of their depth, managing just five wins all season and drawing nine matches at home. Goalscoring was their biggest problem as they netted a mere 29 goals – although the Hornets were desperately unlucky to lose their main striker, Marlon King, to injury at the start of the season. That the club were resigned to their fate became obvious when the exciting Ashley Young was sold to Aston Villa in the January transfer window. It maybe that the pace of the Premiership was also an issue as the Hornets committed more fouls – 597 in all – than any other side. With Watford's regular loss of possession, the opposition found scoring easy. Watford conceded a whopping 59 goals, despite having Manchester United's on-loan and highly regarded keeper Ben Foster between the posts. A Premiership goal difference of –30 was the worst in the League.

Watford had occupied the bottom spot for so much of the campaign it was a grim certainty that they would remain there all season, and their coveted Premiership place was lost by April 21 when they failed to beat Manchester City at home.

Comfort was sought in the FA Cup, where the draw was kinder. They beat Stockport, West Ham, Ipswich and Plymouth before a semi-final clash at Villa Park against Manchester United brought the curtain down for them.

Ebullient manager Adrian Boothroyd remained King Canute-like, endlessly praising his players for their valiant efforts, but it all smacked of 'if wishes were horses, beggars would ride' by the end. But having not spent excessively Watford will be one of the leading lights in the Championship this season.

COACH: ADRIAN BOOTHROYD

Players	Apps	(Subs)	Goals
Moses Ashikodi	21		0
Cedric Avinel	1		0
Alhassan Bangura	12	(4)	0
Hameur Bouazza	26	(5)	5
Clarke Carlisle	4		0
Johan Cavalli	2	(1)	0
Alec Chamberlain	0	(1)	0
James Chambers	8	(4)	0
Jay DeMerit	28	(3)	2
Lloyd Doyley	17	(4)	0
Ben Foster	28		0
Damien Francis	27	(4)	4
Darius Henderson	24	(10)	3
Will Hoskins	4	(5)	0
Albert Jarrett	0	(1)	0
Steven Kabba	6	(5)	0
Marlon King	11	(1)	4
Richard Lee	9	(1)	0
Malky Mackay	12	(1)	0
Gavin Mahon	32	(1)	1
Adrian Mariappa	17	(2)	0
Anthony McNamee	4	(3)	0
Chris Powell	9	(6)	0
Tamas Priskin	7	(9)	2
Douglas Rinaldi	6	(1)	0
Theo Robinson	0	(1)	0
Dan Shittu	26	(3)	1
Tommy Smith	31		1
Matthew Spring	2	(3)	0
Jordan Stewart	29	(1)	0
Gareth Williams	2	(1)	0
Lee Williamson	4	(1)	0
Ashley Young	19		3

A gulf in class: it takes three Hornets to stop a Red Devil in the FA Cup semi-final

At least there was some cheer as Watford managed to score in the 4-1 FA Cup semi-final hammering to United at Villa Park

PREM FACT IT'S ESTIMATED THAT STAYING UP IN THE PREMIERSHIP IS WORTH £30+ MILLION QUID.

Alan Pardew and Arsene Wenger go toe-to-toe

Hammers' Player of the Year and late starter, Carlos Tevez, celebrates with young gun Mark Noble

A change of owners, a change of manager, erratic and bizarre form and a controversial signing that could have been the Hammers' doom… but proved to be the club's saviour – it doesn't get more radical than this!

In August 2006, West Ham signed two of Argentina's World Cup members, Carlos Tevez and Javier Mascherano. Neither player contributed much during the first-half of the season – so much so that Mascherano was off-loaded to Liverpool (and subsequently ended up playing in the Champions League final). Tevez, who had seen more action, had failed to score in 19 games but remained largely confined to the subs' bench.

In November Eggert Magnusson and Bjorgolfur Gudmundsson bought the club for a massive £85 million and in January volunteered copies of transfer documents to the Premier League. It became apparent that in the course of the Tevez and Mascherano transfers, the club had broken rules relating to third-party player ownership. Ultimately, an Independent Premier League Commission would fine West Ham £5.5 million and censure the previous senior club management, but crucially, because the verdict was reached so late in the season, chose not to deduct points. This would have huge implications as a quartet of teams including Sheffield United, Wigan and Charlton fought to avoid relegation.

West Ham now had Alan Curbishley as manager following Alan Pardew's dismissal in December. The former Charlton boss played Tevez more often and saw a transformation in the player that was to prove decisive for the Hammers' survival. The striker, fulfilling the potential he'd shown at the World Cup, proved to be a wicked marksman and inspired the side to a fantastic run of seven wins in their last nine games. Netting seven goals in his final ten games, including the winner at Old Trafford against Manchester United on the last day of the season, helped confirm West Ham's place in the Premiership.

Over the course of the season West Ham were so unpredictable. They twice endured a sequence of five defeats in a row – in fact they lost 21 games in all, more than any other club – yet finished the season in a blaze of glory. They did doubles over leading sides Arsenal and Manchester United but on the flip side lost to Charlton, Sheffield United and Watford, the three clubs relegated to the Championship.

WEST HAM UNITED

BARCLAYS PREMIER LEAGUE: 15th
FA CUP: Fourth Round
CARLING CUP: Third Round
PREMIERSHIP TOP SCORER: Bobby Zamora 11 goals

COACH: ALAN PARDEW; ALAN CURBISHLEY

Players	Apps	(Subs)	Goals
Yossi Benayoun	25	(4)	3
Kepa Blanco	1	(7)	1
Luis Boa Morte	8	(6)	1
Lee Bowyer	18	(2)	0
Roy Carroll	12		0
Carlton Cole	5	(12)	2
James Collins	16		0
Christian Dailly	10	(4)	0
Calum Davenport	5	(1)	0
Matthew Etherington	24	(3)	0
Anton Ferdinand	31		0
Daniel Gabbidon	18		0
Robert Green	26		0
Marlon Harewood	19	(13)	3
Paul Konchesky	22		0
Javier Mascherano	3	(2)	0
George McCartney	16	(6)	0
Tyrone Mears	3	(2)	0
Hayden Mullins	21	(9)	0
Lucas Neill	11		0
Shaun Newton	0	(3)	0
Mark Noble	10		2
John Pantsil	3	(2)	0
Nigel Quashie	7		0
Nigel Reo-Coker	35		1
Teddy Sheringham	4	(13)	2
Jon Spector	17	(8)	0
Carlos Tevez	19	(7)	7
Matthew Upson	2	0	
Bobby Zamora	27	(5)	11

WIGAN ATHLETIC

BARCLAYS PREMIER LEAGUE: 16th
FA CUP: Third Round
CARLING CUP: Second Round
PREMIERSHIP TOP SCORER: Emile Heskey 9 goals

COACH: PAUL JEWELL

Players	Apps	(Subs)	Goals
Julius Aghahowa	3	(3)	0
Leighton Baines	35		3
Emmerson Boyce	34		0
Henri Camara	18	(5)	6
Pascal Chimbonda	0	(1)	0
David Connolly	0	(2)	0
David Cotterill	5	(11)	1
Arjan de Zeeuw	21		0
John Filan	10		0
Caleb Folan	8	(5)	2
Kristofer Haestad	1	(1)	0
Fitz Hall	22	(2)	0
Emile Heskey	33	(1)	9
Matt Jackson	17	(3)	1
Andreas Johansson	4	(7)	0
Graham Kavanagh	0	(2)	0
Kevin Kilbane	26	(5)	1
Chris Kirkland	26		0
Danny Landzaat	29	(4)	2
Lee McCulloch	25	(4)	4
Michael Pollitt	2	(1)	0
Paul Scharner	22	(3)	3
Josip Skoko	24	(4)	0
Ryan Taylor	12	(4)	1
Gary Teale	7	(5)	0
Svetoslav Todorov	2	(3)	0
David Unsworth	6	(4)	1
Antonio Valencia	17	(5)	1
Andy Webster	3	(1)	0
David Wright	6	(6)	0

The agony and the ecstasy: Paul Jewell and Neil Warnock react to the final whistle on the last day of the season

PREM FACT WIGAN ATHLETIC'S MASCOTS JAY-JAY AND BEA ARE INTENTIONALLY NAMED AFTER THE CLUB'S MAIN SPONSOR - JJB

David Unsworth's £30 million penalty

After seven years and 291 games in charge, Wigan boss Paul Jewell resigned less than 24 hours after saving the club from relegation on the final day of the season at Sheffield United. He told the club's website: "I have made this decision with a heavy heart but I feel it is time for me to have a break from football." During his reign Jewell had turned Wigan Athletic from an average League One team to a club that reached its first major final in 2006.

However, the Latics' second season in the top-flight proved a tough one, and their survival in the Premiership would all come down to a must-win game against fellow relegation candidates United at Bramall Lane on the last day of the season. During a dramatic game, Wigan lost captain Arjan de Zeeuw through injury and, in the 74th minute, saw Lee McCulloch sent off. An early lead, scored by the inspiring Paul Scharner, was cancelled out by Jon Stead before a David Unsworth penalty on the stroke of half-time proved to be the winning goal that would keep them in the Premiership.

Just a week before, Wigan had suffered their 20th League defeat of the season and had been dragged into the relegation zone for the first time.

The season had started reasonably well and after 11 games – including four successive wins – they were up in eighth place. The losses then began to pile up including nine successive League and cup defeats during December and January – the worst run of any Premiership side. Wigan slowly began to drop down the table and on the final day they occupied the last relegation spot. The 2-1 win over the Blades was only their 10th win of the season in all competitions but was worth a staggering £30 million to the club – the financial difference between Premiership and Championship football.

WAYNE'S DREAM TEAM PLAYER

Check out my DREAM TEAM on pages 58-63

CRISTIANO RONALDO

MANCHESTER UNITED

WAZZA'S MENTAL CHALLENGE!

Test your footy knowledge with the ultimate Wazza quiz. Answers can be found on page 95

WHICH STRIPS?

So you think you know your European footy? Try matching the strips with these German Bundesliga teams

1

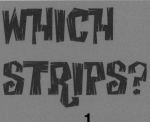

2

3

4

5

ARMINIA BIELEFELD	
ENERGIE COTTBUS	
EINTRACHT FRANKFURT	
BORUSSIA DORTMUND	
VFL WOLFSBURG	

SPOT THE BALL

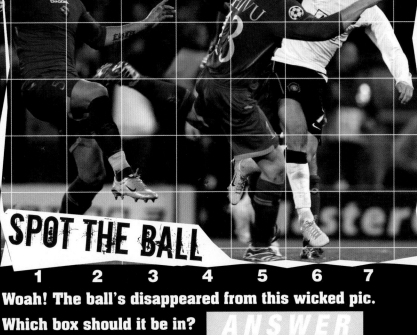

f
e
d
c
b
a

1 2 3 4 5 6 7

Woah! The ball's disappeared from this wicked pic. Which box should it be in?   ANSWER

ALL NATIONS

Which Country do these Manchester United stars come from?

Ji-Sung Park
ANSWER

Gabriel Heinze
ANSWER

Patrice Evra
ANSWER

John O'Shea
ANSWER

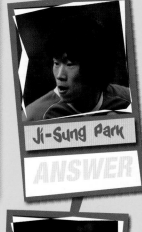
Nemanja Vidic
ANSWER

SUPERSTRIKER

Wayne scored 23 goals for United during the 2006/7 season. How much can you remember about them?

1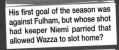
His first goal of the season was against Fulham, but whose shot had keeper Niemi parried that allowed Wazza to slot home?
ANSWER

2
Wayne got a magnificent hat-trick against Bolton on October 28, but how many games had he gone without scoring before then?
ANSWER

3
When Wayne scored against his old club Everton on April 28, who was the rookie keeper in the Everton goal?
ANSWER

4
United's 7-1 demolition of Roma in the Champions League was one of the games of the season. Who supplied the cross for Wazza's goal?
ANSWER

5
Of the 23 goals Wayne scored last season, against which Premiership team did he score his favourite goal?
ANSWER

MY SCORE ..../16

15

WAYNE'S GOALS

Manchester United 5 Fulham 1

WHEN: August 20, 2006

WHERE: Old Trafford

COMPETITION: Premiership

THE LOWDOWN: Cristiano Ronaldo and Man-of-the-Match Rooney teamed up for the first time since their World Cup bust-up and were all smiles as they helped rip apart sorry Fulham with a breathtaking attacking display.

1 GOAL! United were already two up through Louis Saha and an Ian Pearce own goal when Rooney struck in the 16th minute. Cottagers' keeper Antti Niemi had parried a Saha volley but the ball fell to Wayne, who coolly slotted home.

2 GOAL! On 64 minutes, Paul Scholes fed the overlapping Wes Brown, who pulled the ball back for Rooney – who incidentally set up Ronaldo for the fourth – to shoot low into the corner.

WHAT WAYNE SAID: "People who don't know Cristiano and I have said a lot about us this summer but we let our football do the talking today. At times Fulham couldn't live with us, which is a credit to all the players. We know the quality we have here in the squad and as long as we stay focused. I think we'll be up there."

WHAT THEY SAID: "You could tell Cristiano and Wayne are the best of pals. They linked up together on numerous occasions. People always look for scapegoats but we have a great spirit here and we will not let that be affected by what people say outside the club." Sir Alex Ferguson

"HIS TOUCH AND TIMING MADE IT A BRILLIANT GOAL"

Bolton W 0 Manchester United 4

WHEN: October 28, 2006

WHERE: Reebok Stadium

COMPETITION: Premiership

THE LOWDOWN: After a 10-game goal drought, Wayne took his frustrations out on Bolton with a stunning hat-trick as United continued their best-ever start to a Premiership season.

3 GOAL! Wayne opened his account on 10 minutes, latching on to an inch-perfect Michael Carrick pass before lashing the ball home with his left foot from 12 yards.

4 GOAL! Rooney made it two just six minutes later, picking up a deflected pass from Gary Neville before delightfully curling the ball past Wanderers keeper Jussi Jaaskelainen from the edge of the box.

5 GOAL! Rooney's first hat-trick since his United debut against Fenerbache arrived on 89 minutes when he picked up Darren Fletcher's pass with a lovely touch before rifling the ball home.

WHAT THEY SAID: "Wayne Rooney has proved beyond doubt that he's the best English player in the Premiership. His hat-trick was well deserved and it just shows the people who were writing him off were talking nonsense." Bolton boss Sam Allardyce

Holland 1 England 1

WHEN: November 15, 2006

WHERE: Amsterdam Arena

COMPETITION: Friendly International

THE LOWDOWN: Following his World Cup frustrations, Wayne scored his first England goal in more than a year, but the Dutch grabbed a share of the spoils thanks to Rafael van der Vaart's 86th minute equaliser.

GOAL! England took the lead eight minutes before half-time when Joe Cole's deep right-wing cross was instinctively volleyed home by Rooney at the far post. It was his first goal since the friendly win against Argentina in Geneva.

WHAT THEY SAID: "We all know about Wazza's quality and he took his goal brilliantly. There's not a defender in the world who can enjoy marking him." England skipper John Terry

6

"ROONEY IS THE BEST ENGLISH PLAYER IN THE PREM"

Sheff United 1 Manchester United 2

WHEN: November 18, 2006

WHERE: Bramall Lane

COMPETITION: Premiership

THE LOWDOWN: Struggling United took a surprise lead through ex-Red Keith Gillespie, but a goal in either half by Rooney took his tally to six goals in seven matches.

7

GOAL! United grabbed their equaliser after 30 minutes when Gary Neville delivered the ball into the box. Rooney, who had got between defenders Phil Jagielka and Claude Davis, controlled the ball with his left foot before burying it with his right from eight yards out.

8

GOAL! Patrice Evra broke forward and his left wing cross dropped over the head of defender Davis, leaving Wayne to fire a first-time shot across the bows of Blades keeper Paddy Kenny and into the back of the net.

WHAT WAYNE SAID: "I knew that once I got games under my belt I'd be back to my best and over the last month I've shown that. Of the two, I liked the first goal more because it got us back level in the game and I don't score that many in the centre of the goal."

WHAT THEY SAID: "They were two marvellous finishes from Rooney. The first came from a run across the defender. He has caught him on the hop, off-guard, and it was a great strike. The second was terrific. Taking that kind of finish, when you are under pressure and you need to win, it makes it more special." Sir Alex Ferguson

WAYNE'S GOALS

Manchester United 3 Man City 1

WHEN: December 9, 2006

WHERE: Old Trafford

COMPETITION: Premiership

THE LOWDOWN: United extended their lead over Chelsea at the top of the table to nine points. Wayne opened the scoring after just six minutes, while Gabriel Heinze and Cristiano Ronaldo also got themselves on the scoresheet to make it a happy day against their Manchester rivals.

9 GOAL! Ronaldo's cross from the right rolled embarrassingly under the outstretched leg of City defender Sylvain Distin and Rooney was on hand to slot a perfect side-foot finish past goalkeeper Nicky Weaver.

WHAT THEY SAID: "In these games you've got to punish any mistakes the opposition make and we did that with three very well taken goals. It was good to get an early goal through Wayne as it settled us down and we created plenty of chances from then on." Ryan Giggs

> "WAYNE ROONEY IS UP THERE WITH THE BEST I HAVE EVER PLAYED WITH"

Arsenal 2 Manchester United 1

WHEN: January 21, 2007

WHERE: Emirates Stadium

COMPETITION: Premiership

THE LOWDOWN: United remained six points clear of Chelsea despite throwing away victory in this 200th fixture against their north London rivals. Rooney had handed the visitors the lead before Arsenal equalised on 83 minutes through Robin van Persie. The Gunners then snatched victory when Thierry Henry pounced with an injury-time header.

10 GOAL: Eight minutes after the re-start, Patrice Evra broke down the left for United and his low cross was met at the far post by the on-rushing Rooney, who drilled home past Jens Lehmann for only his second goal in 14 games.

WHAT THEY SAID: "Wayne has given us a deserved lead then we lost two goals from a position I did not think we would. At this moment in time we are so disappointed, but we have a game less to play and are a goal better off than Chelsea so it is not all doom and gloom." Sir Alex Ferguson

Manchester United 2 Pompey 1

WHEN: January 27, 2007

WHERE: Old Trafford

COMPETITION: FA Cup Round 4

THE LOWDOWN: Having come off the bench, two late Rooney goals in a devastating six-minute spell booked United's place in round five against a spirited Portsmouth side.

11 GOAL! Rooney opened the scoring in the 77th minute when he side-footed home a low Ryan Giggs cross from six yards out.

12 GOAL! Receiving the ball 30 yards out, Rooney accelerated forward and drew his foot back as if to unleash a thunderbolt shot. Instead, he exquisitely chipped the ball over bewildered David James and into the back of the net.

WHAT WAYNE SAID: "To come off the bench and score two goals, I'm delighted with that but even more pleased that we don't have to go back to Fratton Park for a replay. For the second goal, I turned and was looking for a pass but couldn't see one. So I went for the chip and it went in. But I was just as pleased with the first goal because I need to get a few more of those 'easy' goals. The FA Cup is something I dreamed of winning since a kid. I got close two years ago, so hopefully I can go one better this time."

WHAT THEY SAID: "Having the vision and audacity to do it at that time in the game is really great. It was nice to get Wayne scoring and the chip really was world class. I remember Eric Cantona doing that in the FA Cup against Sheffield United."
Sir Alex Ferguson

"NO DEFENDER ENJOYS MARKING WAZZA"

Manchester United 4 Watford 0

WHEN: January 31, 2007

WHERE: Old Trafford

COMPETITION: Premiership

THE LOWDOWN: United made it nine straight wins at home, against basement boys Watford. Ronaldo opened the account with a first-half penalty, before the hosts stepped on the gas with three goals in ten blockbusting second-half minutes.

13 GOAL! United saved their best till last when Ronaldo scooped his 71st minute pass up and over the Watford defence. Rooney then showed great awareness to latch onto the bouncing ball before lobbing it over advancing goalkeeper Richard Lee for his fourth goal in three games.

WHAT THEY SAID: "Wayne Rooney is up there with the best I have ever played with. He has the vision, he can score goals and he is a great passer of the ball. It's fantastic to be able to play in a team with players like him."
On-loan team-mate Henrik Larsson.

17

M'boro 2 Manchester United 2

WHEN: March 10, 2007

WHERE: The Riverside

COMPETITION: FA Cup round six

THE LOWDOWN: Rooney had given United the lead but goals either side of half-time from Middlesbrough midfielders Lee Cattermole and George Boateng put the hosts in the driving seat. Ronaldo salvaged a replay with a 68th minute penalty.

GOAL! Ryan Giggs fed Rooney and after taking a couple of touches, he drove the ball low past Boro keeper Mark Schwarzer to hand United a 23rd minute lead.

WHAT THEY SAID: "Wayne got us into the lead but we had to work hard and was helped because the spirit here is unbelievable. You don't become a great team by playing pretty football and winning well every week. You have to grind out results and show character." Michael Carrick

Manchester United 4 Bolton W 1

WHEN: March 17, 2007

WHERE: Old Trafford

COMPETITION: Premiership

THE LOWDOWN: United remained six points clear at the top of the table thanks to two superb strikes from Rooney and another brace from Ji-Sung Park. But it was Cristiano Ronaldo who stole the show, having had a hand in three of the goals.

GOAL! Already 1-0 up and with 17 minutes on the clock, Ronaldo picked up the ball in his own penalty area and following a one-two with Rooney, the pair set off on a surging run forward. Having reached the edge of Bolton's penalty area, Ronaldo squared the ball left for Rooney, who delightfully chipped the ball over the advancing Jussi Jaaskelainen from 10 yards. It was one of the defining moments of the season.

GOAL! Sub Alan Smith picked up the ball mid-way inside his own half before sending Rooney clear with a delightful pass on 74 minutes. With only the keeper to beat, Wayne smashed the ball into the top corner of the net from 12 yards.

WHAT THEY SAID: "Cristiano's had an incredible season and his combination with Wayne Rooney for the second goal was tremendous." Sir Alex Ferguson

Roma 2 Manchester United 1

WHEN: April 4, 2007

WHERE: Stadio Olimpico, Rome

COMPETITION: Champions League quarter-final, first leg

THE LOWDOWN: Despite a red card for Paul Scholes after just 33 minutes of the game, Rooney kept United's Champions League dreams alive with his first goal in the competition since September 2004.

GOAL! With an hour gone and United a goal down, Ronaldo found Ole Solskjaer with a superb pass. The Norwegian then sent over a far-post cross to Rooney who chested down, lost his marker and lashed home his first Champions League goal since his debut against Fenerbache.

WHAT WAYNE SAID: "There has been a lot of talk about the fact I have not scored for a while in the Champions League. Hopefully now the talking will stop and I can concentrate on trying to get more goals. I don't know why I had not scored. I have had chances. Maybe I should have scored on some occasions, on others the keeper has made good saves, but obviously, it is a relief to finally get the goal."

WHAT THEY SAID: "The great thing what Rooney showed was that for a boy of 21 he showed great composure in front of goal. In a big occasion like today, he could have hit it straight away, but he composed himself, side-stepped the defender and finished well." Sir Alex Ferguson

WAYNE'S GOALS

ONE OF THE GREATEST PERFORMANCES
IN THE HISTORY OF THE CLUB

Manchester United 7 Roma 1

WHEN: April 10, 2007

WHERE: Old Trafford

COMPETITION: Champions League quarter-final, second leg

THE LOWDOWN: In one of the greatest performances in the history of the club, United completely blew away Roma to set up a semi-final showdown with AC Milan. Rooney scored the all-important third, after just 19 minutes, and United had netted six of their incredible seven goals inside an hour.

GOAL! Ryan Giggs ripped Roma apart down their left flank and his low, drilled cross was slotted home at the far post by Rooney, who had timed his run to absolute perfection.

WHAT THEY SAID: "This points the way ahead. Two years ago when we played against AC Milan, Wayne Rooney and Cristiano Ronaldo were young boys but they showed they've grown up tonight." Sir Alex Ferguson

18

Manchester United 4 Watford 1

WHEN: April 14, 2007

WHERE: Villa Park

COMPETITION: FA Cup semi-final

THE LOWDOWN: Rooney inspired United to glory with the first and third goals against plucky Watford. The victory set up a showdown with Chelsea in the first FA Cup final to be staged at the new Wembley Stadium.

19 **GOAL!** Rooney opened the scoring on seven minutes, picking up Michael Carrick's pass out on the left, then side-stepping defender Adrian Mariappa before thundering a shot pass Richard Lee, who barely moved.

20 **GOAL!** The third goal, on 66 minutes, came against the run of play when Rooney tapped in a cross by Alan Smith after Clarke Carlisle had initially denied him.

WHAT WAYNE SAID: "This was a big performance by us. We had to dig in deep because we've had a lot of games lately. Our second goal was crucial as it came just after they had equalised and were putting us under pressure with some high balls. But I like this ground, I've scored a few goals here."

WHAT THEY SAID: "Wayne Rooney had his best game of the season, he was absolutely fantastic. But it was a fantastic performance all round. I was so proud." Sir Alex Ferguson

21

Manchester United 2 Sheffield United 0

WHEN: April 17, 2007

WHERE: Old Trafford

COMPETITION: Premiership

THE LOWDOWN: United closed in on the title with a comfortable win over a Blades side deep in relegation trouble. Michael Carrick grabbed a fourth minute lead before Rooney scored the all-important second just five minutes after the re-start. The win again put the heat on Chelsea.

21 GOAL! Ryan Giggs clipped over a delightful pass that Rooney brought down with the outside of his right boot before lashing an unstoppable shot that flew across the despairing dive of Blades keeper Paddy Kenny.

WHAT THEY SAID: "While we were always in control of the game, Sheffield United were defending in numbers, so Wayne getting the second goal so soon after the break gave us that little bit of daylight." Ryan Giggs

Manchester United 3 AC Milan 2

WHEN: April 24, 2007

WHERE: Old Trafford

COMPETITION: Champions League semi-final, first leg

THE LOWDOWN: Rooney scored twice, including a stunning last-minute winner, to keep United's hopes of reaching the final alive. He grabbed the headlines along with Brazilian playmaker Kaka, who also netted twice on the night for Milan.

22 GOAL! With United losing 2-1 and almost an hour on the clock, Paul Scholes played a delightful ball through to Rooney and having brought the ball down on his chest, he drove past the spread-eagled Milan keeper Dida.

23 GOAL! Rooney won a tackle to start the attack. The ball eventually fell to Ryan Giggs, who whipped in a trademark cross and Wayne was there, opening up his body to drive the ball past Dida at the near post.

WHAT WAYNE SAID: "We kept going to the end. We knew that if we could get a victory here, it will be easier when we go to the away leg."

WHAT THEY SAID: "As we were putting the ball out wide to try and stretch them, Wayne wasn't having the greatest involvement but when he was getting the ball, he was a threat to them. In the second half he was dropping off to beat men, winning free-kicks and, of course, scoring the winning goal which was incredible. His touch and timing made it a brilliant goal." Sir Alex Ferguson

Everton 2 Manchester United 4

WHEN: April 28, 2007

WHERE: Goodison Park

COMPETITION: Premiership

THE LOWDOWN: United battled back from two goals down to win the game, leaving them just 24 hours from winning the Premiership crown. Rooney netted United's all-important third goal on 79 minutes against his former club.

24 GOAL! With United hunting for a third goal, it arrived when Wayne brought down John O'Shea's cross on the left-hand side of the box. He then shimmied past Tony Hibbert's desperate lunge, before drilling home a delightful right-foot shot past Alan Stubbs and rookie keeper Iain Turner.

WHAT THEY SAID: "The thing that always gives me hope is these players really want to win every game. They're all out to score, all the time. When I see the camaraderie and the team spirit and the desire I can go to bed at night knowing I've got a good group of players." Sir Alex Ferguson

WAYNE'S GOALS

AMSTERDAM
AMSTERDAM ARENA

1 GOAL SCORED

AMSTERDAM

MANCHESTER
OLD TRAFFORD

12 GOALS SCORED

MIDDLESBROUGH

MIDDLESBROUGH
RIVERSIDE STADIUM

1 GOAL SCORED

BOLTON
REEBOK STADIUM

3 GOALS SCORED

BOLTON

MANCHESTER

LIVERPOOL
GOODISON PARK

1 GOAL SCORED

LIVERPOOL

SHEFFIELD

SHEFFIELD
BRAMALL LANE

2 GOALS SCORED

BIRMINGHAM

BIRMINGHAM
VILLA PARK

2 GOALS SCORED

LONDON

LONDON
EMIRATES STADIUM

1 GOAL SCORED

ROME
STADIO OLIMPICO

1 GOAL SCORED

ROME

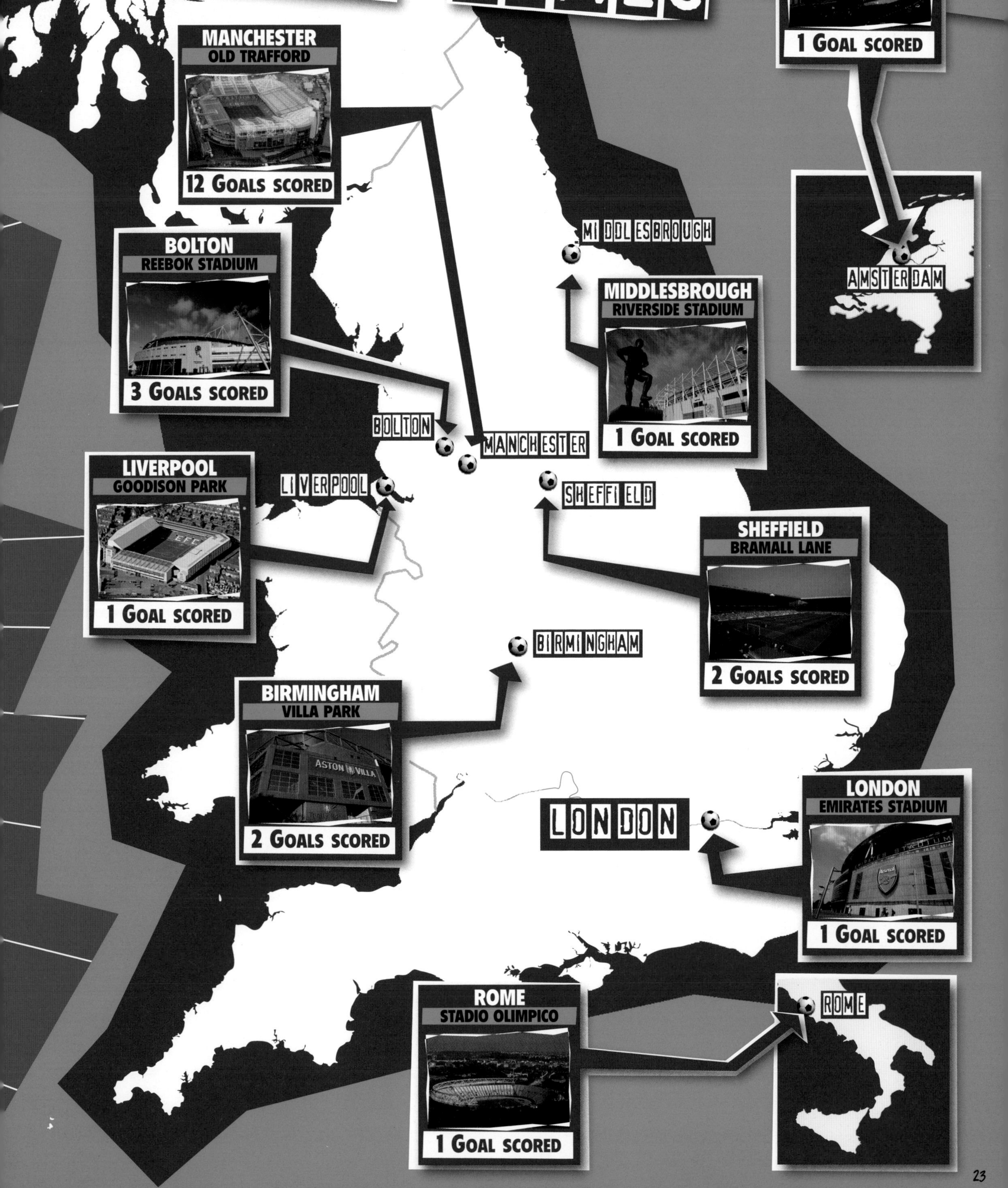

PETR CECH
CHELSEA

SAMSUNG
mobile

WAYNE'S
DREAM TEAM
PLAYER

Check out my DREAM TEAM on pages 58-63

WAZZA'S MENTAL CHALLENGE! 2

We never said that Wazza's quiz would be easy! Answers can be found on page 95

GUESS THE PLAYER
[as the Lone Ranger]

We've missed one name out just to make it tougher!

Steven Gerrard

Dimitar Berbatov

Wes Brown   Kaka

2 ANSWER

3 ANSWER

4 ANSWER

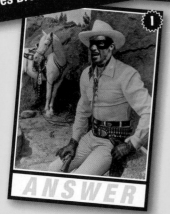
5 ANSWER

1 ANSWER

WAZZA'S PLAYER SEARCH!

THERE ARE 33 HIDDEN PLAYERS IN THE PLAYER SEARCH BELOW! CAN YOU FIND THEM ALL?

H	F	Y	Z	Q	R	S	V	S	I	L	V	E	S	T	R	E	X	G	K	N	B	O	S
N	P	S	L	U	Y	Y	T	D	A	F	J	A	C	E	Q	A	S	C	V	F	G	Z	N
A	O	S	T	F	L	E	T	C	H	E	R	P	X	S	P	G	Y	G	J	L	S	E	B
Y	X	N	K	E	J	K	I	W	S	D	H	B	O	V	S	L	Q	P	N	C	H	D	F
Q	D	P	A	R	K	X	C	K	Z	P	P	T	S	J	D	E	X	Y	E	A	P	B	X
R	A	D	X	D	F	S	D	X	Z	U	Q	B	H	W	W	S	F	C	V	D	S	A	P
P	F	Y	Q	I	Z	Q	R	H	E	I	N	Z	E	X	K	N	G	Y	I	B	C	R	S
F	X	A	D	N	H	O	Q	A	P	Z	R	R	A	Y	X	V	V	T	L	J	K	N	Y
Z	R	R	K	A	N	D	E	R	S	O	N	V	Y	T	T	P	N	S	L	W	Z	E	C
L	S	X	O	N	P	P	F	G	X	P	C	S	O	L	S	K	J	A	E	R	K	S	J
V	H	C	P	D	Z	R	Y	R	S	G	W	F	R	S	V	Z	A	C	P	I	P	L	I
Z	A	T	V	J	L	K	J	E	P	I	U	Y	T	S	F	H	K	L	G	C	V	B	N
M	W	F	T	A	H	G	I	A	G	K	L	A	S	D	F	G	H	C	B	H	J	E	B
W	C	K	R	U	P	S	Z	V	A	N	D	E	R	S	A	R	X	P	G	A	V	D	G
Y	R	K	S	D	V	T	Y	E	G	V	D	C	H	A	Q	O	D	F	G	R	Z	S	P
Q	O	X	Z	G	I	G	G	S	W	R	T	Y	U	H	X	N	Z	V	B	D	O	N	G
E	S	B	C	B	D	F	H	J	K	B	V	R	Z	A	K	A	I	Y	B	S	F	H	X
Z	S	X	S	M	I	T	H	V	B	D	H	A	F	B	S	L	W	E	V	O	E	V	Z
K	X	F	G	R	C	D	F	B	S	N	R	T	Y	X	V	D	R	T	R	N	Q	X	V
D	G	H	X	S	B	U	Z	X	F	A	Y	B	G	B	R	O	W	N	H	G	D	N	U
C	V	F	K	S	T	G	Q	W	C	N	F	S	H	J	O	F	H	J	K	C	B	N	F
D	F	O	Q	P	C	R	V	B	N	I	X	S	C	H	O	L	E	S	K	W	E	B	V
K	U	S	Z	C	Z	A	K	C	V	G	E	P	A	M	N	F	S	D	R	U	I	B	X
B	T	T	S	D	B	Y	X	C	D	F	F	W	R	J	E	V	R	A	X	B	F	D	H
L	E	E	V	V	G	T	R	R	P	Z	D	V	R	X	Y	S	D	G	J	K	I	X	V
Z	T	R	P	J	F	S	B	X	F	H	H	J	I	W	E	D	D	F	G	J	L	B	M
D	F	G	C	B	Y	T	E	R	U	N	Z	B	C	A	T	H	C	A	R	T	Q	H	J
O	D	M	A	R	T	I	N	B	B	F	G	S	K	D	F	W	G	G	C	H	U	I	X
A	S	F	G	K	J	J	E	Y	Y	D	U	Z	X	E	Y	K	M	D	G	B	W	G	J

Van der Sar	Silvestre	Saha	Gray	Scholes
Heinze	Cathcart	Park	Martin	Dong
Ronaldo	Lee	Carrick	Hargreaves	Fletcher
Giggs	Barnes	Richardson	Evra	Shawcross
Vidic	Anderson	Solskjaer	Brown	Nani
Foster	Neville	Kuszczak	Rooney	
O'Shea	Ferdinand	Eagles	Smith	

GUESS THE STRIKE PARTNER

ANSWER

NUMBER 10s

Wayne will wear the illustrious number 10 shirt for United this season. Can you match these legends of the game who have all worn the famous shirt with their former clubs?

- Dennis Bergkamp ☐
- Diego Maradona ☐
- Zinedine Zidane ☐
- Pele ☐
- Geoff Hurst ☐

A - Ajax   B - Sevilla   C - Bordeaux
D - New York Cosmos   E - Stoke City

MY SCORE ..../44

25

WAYNE'S BIG

Wayne has been getting some stick from his team-mates about his golfing skills lately, so one day after training he heads off to the local club to practise. But the afternoon's events don't quite turn out as expected. . .

Yo soy Sergio Ramos y soy de Madrid.

Excelente! There is my friend Wazzo. He will teach me this game.

Eat your heart out Nevo.

This is easy peasy. I'll soon be able to take all the lads on.

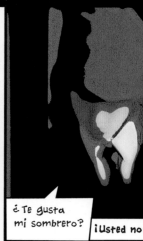

¿Te gusta mi sombrero?

¡Usted no

Este es un juego muy estupido, me voy a casa.

¿Que debemos hacer ahora?

Soy un futbolista excelente reconocido mundialmente.

Plays for Real Madrid? More like the Royal Oak!

Definitivamente estuvo fuera de juego.

One touch and get rid, Wazza.

Both Sergio Ramos Garcia and Wayne Rooney are players featured in the world's best-selling footy game, FIFA 08.

Real Madrid signed Sergio from Sevilla for €27 million (about £18 million) in the summer of 2005 – the second most expensive teenager after Wayne and Spain's most expensive domestic signing. Sergio usually plays at the centre of defence for Real and is known for his perseverance, powerful shots, crosses, long-ball passes and heading ability. He made his debut for the Spanish senior side at only 19 years of age, making him the youngest player to play for the national team in the last 55 years. He held this record until it was broken by Arsenal's Cesc Fábregas.

SPANISH TRANSLATION

Yo soy Sergio Ramos y soy de Madrid.
I am Sergio Ramos and I am from Madrid.

¿Te gusta mi sombrero?
Do you like my hat?

DAY OUT!

EPISODE #1

FIFA 08

has taken football gaming to a whole new level. It now plays like the real thing, so that you need to 'feel' the ball and play with natural skill and flair. And who better than big FIFA fan Wazza to have his game modelled by the EA's boffins, so that millions of game players all over the planet can play just like him!

Can you imagine how weird it must feel picking up the game controller to play the game as yourself! Wayne says, "I always play as United and I always try to give the ball to me and score. I've scored a few more headers on that than I have in real life!."

Wayne spent ages with EA's top game designers making sure every nuance of his game was properly captured. "They attached a load of sensors to me and recorded my movements. It was actually more difficult to do the skills when people are telling you what to do; when you're doing it on the pitch, it's far more instinctive. But it was great and I really enjoyed meself."

On away trips, Wayne often finds himself competing with Manchester United team-mate and FIFA master Darren Fletcher.

"He just sits in the house all day practising. I won't let him play as United against me, though. If I'm United, the other player can't be United and control me! He usually goes for Arsenal."

WIN EA SPORTS FIFA 08

EA SPORTS™

THERE ARE FIVE COPIES OF FIFA 08 TO BE WON. TURN TO PAGE 49 FOR DETAILS.

27

perfect number 10

If you want to class yourself a true footballing great, then you simply have to wear the cherished number ten shirt. It's the shirt worn by the legends of the game and the shirt that Wayne Rooney has proudly decided to call his own from now on at Manchester United.

But what's so special about the number ten, you might ask. After all it's just a number? Well let's get one thing straight from the start, ten is more than just a number. In football, it's a symbol of greatness, and is reserved for those select few players who have that something extra in their locker. Be it a midfield maestro, or a goalscoring great, if you've got it, then you can most definitely flaunt it.

And what company Rooney now finds himself in! From the greats of the past, like Pele, Platini and Maradona, through to the modern-day wonders of Ronaldinho and Zidane, they've all performed their box of tricks with the magic number ten sitting proudly on their backs.

It's the shirt that sets you apart from the rest, the shirt that means you're the best, and as Wayne steps out onto the pitch this season with his new number sitting proudly under his name, he'll be joining this elite group of Ten-Tastic players...

THE STORY: Hurst made his name with local club West Ham United, helping the Hammers to FA Cup success against Preston in 1964 and European Cup Winners' Cup glory against 1860 Munich a year later. Having netted in both matches, his big-game reputation attracted the attention of England boss Alf Ramsey and a debut arrived against West Germany in February 1966. Five months later, against the same opposition, he became a World Cup legend by netting a hat-trick in the final at Wembley and his world changed forever. Hurst went on to make 499 appearances for the Hammers, netting 252 goals, while his record in an England shirt was equally impressive with 24 goals in 49 appearances. He wound down his career with spells at Stoke, West Brom and the Seattle Sounders in America, and was knighted in 1998.

Name: Geoff Hurst
Born: December 8, 1941
Clubs: West Ham, Stoke City, West Brom, Seattle Sounders
Country: England
Career record: 602 games, 245 goals

Mega career highlight: Hurst went into the 1966 World Cup finals as only a squad member, playing second fiddle to Jimmy Greaves and Roger Hunt. Indeed, the pair were picked for the group games against Uruguay, Mexico and France, only for Greaves to pick up a shin injury against the French. Up stepped Hurst for the quarter-finals with Argentina, the semi with Portugal and then for the 4-2 final victory against West Germany. His hat-trick that afternoon – including *that* hotly-disputed second when the ball bounced down off the crossbar and seemingly over the line – is regarded as the perfect hat-trick as he netted with his left foot, right foot and his head. If that wasn't cool enough, he remains the only player to have scored three goals in a World Cup final. The closest England have since come to the final was a semi-final defeat to the Germans in 1990.

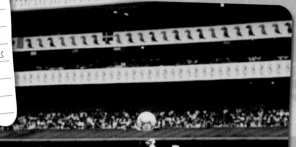

Name: Diego Maradona
Born: October 30, 1960
Clubs: Argentinos Juniors, Boca Juniors, Barcelona, Napoli, Sevilla, Newell's Old Boys
Country: Argentina
Career record: 580 games, 292 goals

Mega career highlight: While he drew huge controversy for his 'Hand of God' first goal against England (above), his second in the 2-1 quarter-final win at Mexico 86 is regarded by many as the greatest of all time. Having picked up the ball in his own half, he swivelled before running more than half the length of the field, skipping past Glenn Hoddle, Peter Reid, Kenny Sansom, Terry Butcher and Terry Fenwick before tucking the ball past keeper Peter Shilton.

THE STORY: Regarded as the best player of the past 30 years and, for many, the greatest player of all time, Maradona became a world superstar when he joined Barcelona for a then-world record fee of £5m in 1982. While his time at the Nou Camp was unspectacular, he emerged as the greatest player on the planet when he joined Napoli in 1984 and single-handedly dragged the Italian strugglers off the floor to Serie A titles in 1987 and 1990, likewise a Uefa Cup win in 1989. Yet it was his exploits for Argentina that really set him apart, most notably at the 1986 World Cup when he all but won the tournament on his own. His amazing dribbling skills, eye for goal, and high energy levels, all aided by a low centre of gravity, made him pretty much unplayable that summer and although he later suffered many off-field problems, he will always be remembered for what he achieved on the football pitch.

Name: Zinedine Zidane
Born: June 23, 1972
Clubs: Cannes, Bordeaux, Juventus, Real Madrid
Country: France
Career record: 610 games, 126 goals

THE STORY: The most technically gifted player of the modern era, 'Zizou' emerged as a true great when he led Juventus to Serie A titles in 1997 and 1998. As Marcello Lippi's main man, he put fellow midfielders Edgar Davids and Didier Deschamps firmly in the shade with his trickery, vision and spectacular free-kicks. It was a golden era for Zidane as he also helped France to World Cup glory in 1998 and European Championship success two years later. His tag as the world's best prompted Real Madrid to splash out a mind-blowing £46.5m for his services in 2001 and he repaid a big chunk of the fee by scoring a blockbuster winning volley against Bayer Leverkusen in the Champions League final that season. Zidane also won a La Liga title for Madrid before controversially bowing out of football with his headbutt on Marco Materazzi as France lost the 2006 World Cup final to Italy. But with three World Player of the Year awards under his belt, the glory far outweighs the controversy.

Mega career highlight: Zidane became a national hero as his two goals against holders Brazil helped France to a 3-0 victory in the 1998 World Cup final. In what was billed as a closely-contested game, Zizou was the difference, powering home two headers, both from corners, in the 26th minute and first-half injury time. Arsenal's Emmanuel Petit wrapped the game up in stoppage time, but there was only one name on the lips of the Parisians who celebrated in their millions in the streets afterwards.

Name: Pele
Born: October 23, 1940
Clubs: Santos, New York Cosmos
Country: Brazil
Career record: 763 games, 707 goals

THE STORY: Pele, or Edson Arantes do Nascimento to give him his full name, was known as the King of Football during his playing days and many people rate him above Maradona as the greatest player of all time. If his official goalscoring record is anything to go by, he stands alone, although his critics state that he never really tested himself against Europe's best teams, having played for the majority of his career with Brazilian giants Santos. However, Pele responded to his doubters by becoming the only footballer to have played in three World Cup-winning teams, netting 12 goals in 14 games in the process. His eye for the extraordinary and ability to skip past players as if they weren't there was unlike anything ever seen before on the world stage. In December 2000 he was named Player of the Century by FIFA, much to the annoyance of one Maradona!

Mega career highlight: The 1970 World Cup finals in Mexico was Pele's last tournament but also his most glorious. Having led Brazil to the final against Italy, he netted the opening goal of the game, rising high to head the ball over defender Tarcisio Burgnich and into the back of the net. He then set up two more goals for Jairzinho and Carlos Alberto, the latter one regarded as the greatest World Cup goal ever, given the wonderful build-up play which led to the goal. Burgnich, who marked Pele during the match, was quoted as saying: "I told myself before the game, he's made of skin and bones just like everyone else — but I was wrong."

THE STORY: Regarded as the most technically gifted player of his generation in Serie A, Baggio is the only Italian to score for his country in three World Cups. He emerged on the world stage following 39 goals in 94 games at Fiorentina and his £7.7m move to Juventus in 1990 was a world record at the time. He helped Juve to the Uefa Cup in 1993 and the Scudetto in 1995, before joining AC Milan where he won the title again the following season. Baggio is unfortunately remembered for missing the all-important spot kick for Italy which helped Brazil win the 1994 World Cup (below), but it should be remembered that he single-handedly got the Italians to that final and he netted 27 goals in 56 games for his country.

Name: Roberto Baggio
Born: February 18, 1967
Clubs: Vicenza, Fiorentina, Juventus, AC Milan, Bologna, Inter Milan, Brescia
Country: Italy
Career record: 545 games, 245 goals

Mega career highlight: In the semi-finals of the 1994 World Cup, Italy faced surprise package Bulgaria and Baggio, dubbed 'The Divine Ponytail' for his haircut that summer, netted both goals in a 2-1 win. He opened the account on 20 minutes, scoring exquisitely from a Roberto Donadoni centre, then doubled the lead five minutes later. There was, however, a price to pay as he injured his leg that day and failed to find his true form in the final defeat against Brazil.

Name: Denis Law
Born: February 24, 1940
Clubs: Huddersfield, Manchester City, Torino, Manchester United
Country: Scotland
Career record: 558 games, 265 goals

THE STORY: There was a time in the 1960s when Manchester United boasted, arguably, the three best players on the planet in George Best, Denis Law and Bobby Charlton. Yet only one of them wore the number ten shirt - The Lawman! Having started his career with Huddersfield Town, Manchester City signed Denis for a British record fee of £55,000 in 1960 but just a year later he was on his way to Italian side Torino for £110,000 - which was a new record fee between an English and Italian club. He failed to settle in Italy and returned to Manchester in 1962, this time with United for another record fee of £115,000. In 11 glorious years at Old Trafford he scored 236 goals in 409 appearances. The Scot was crowned European Footballer of the Year in 1964 and helped United to the league title in 1965 and 1967. He left United in 1973 for a return to Manchester City, but remains United's second highest goalscorer behind Charlton to this day.

Mega career highight: Cruelly injury meant Denis Law missed United's famous European Cup triumph in 1968, but he readily admits that the greatest moment of his career had come five seasons earlier in the 1963 FA Cup final against Leicester City. Believe it or not in those days Leicester were favourites to win, but Law opened the scoring for Manchester United after half-an-hour, swivelling to shoot past Gordon Banks, and then continued to terrorise the City defence for the remainder of the game. David Herd also scored twice as United romped to a 3-1 win, but it was Denis Law who walked away with the man-of-the-match award.

Name: Michel Platini
Born: June 21, 1955
Clubs: AC Nancy, St Etienne, Juventus
Country: France
Career record: 501 games, 265 goals

Mega career highlight: Platini stole the show at the 1984 European Championships in the same way Maradona sprinkled his magic on the 1986 World Cup. He netted two hat-tricks along the way to the final but never was he more impressive than in an epic semi-final against Portugal. Jean-Francois Domergue handed the hosts a first-half lead with a deflected free-kick, only for Rui Jordao to equalise after 74 minutes. The Portuguese then took a shock lead in extra-time, through Jordao, only for Platini to step up to the plate and set up Domergue for an equaliser with six minutes remaining. With the seconds counting down to penalties, the French then broke down the right through Jean Tigana and his low cross was met by Platini who stabbed home for a breathtaking victory.

THE STORY: For an attacking midfielder, Platini had a wonderful goalscoring record. Many of best strikes were trademark free-kicks and having netted a cool 156 goals in 282 games during his time in France, he joined Serie A giants Juventus in 1982. As the main man for 'The Old Lady' Platini won the Scudetto twice in 1984 and 1986, which was sandwiched between a European Cup victory against Liverpool. He finished the division's top scorer in three consecutive seasons and if that wasn't enough, he won a hat-trick of European Footballer of the Year awards. In a bulging cabinet of silverware, Platini also skippered his country to the 1984 European Championships, finishing the tournament as top-scorer with nine goals. He is now President of Uefa.

Name: Dennis Bergkamp
Born: May 10, 1969
Clubs: Ajax, Inter Milan, Arsenal
Country: Holland
Career record: 631 games, 238 goals

THE STORY: One of the Premier League's all-time greatest foreign players, alongside Eric Cantona, Gianfranco Zola and Thierry Henry, 'The Iceman' brought style and grace to an Arsenal team that, before his arrival, had become known for its long-ball football and dull 1-0 victories. He started his career with home-town club Ajax, netting 122 goals in 239 games, and winning Dutch League and Uefa Cup honours, before a move to Italian giants Inter Milan in 1993. While he won the Uefa Cup for a second time, he never settled in Serie A, and moved to Arsenal for £7.5m in 1995. Following Arsene Wenger's arrival a year later, Bergkamp became a pivotal member of the side, and his creativity and goals contributed to three Premier League and four FA Cup successes before his retirement from the game in 2006.

Mega career highlight: At the 1998 World Cup in France, Bergkamp scored the winning goal as Holland overcame Argentina in the quarter-finals. Having lept into the air to control Frank de Boer's 60-yard pass, Bergy brought the ball down through Roberto Ayala's legs before volleying home with the outside of his right foot from a tight angle.

THE STORY: Now regarded as one of the Premiership's most established managers, Blackburn gaffer Hughes was a Manchester United goalscoring legend following two successful spells at the club. Having made his debut in 1983, 'Sparky' became a key player in the side which won the 1985 FA Cup final and he netted a cool 57 goals in 89 appearances before joining Barcelona, along with Gary Lineker, in 1986. Unfortunately he failed to settle in Terry Venables' side and following a loan spell with Bayern Munich, he returned to Old Trafford in May 1988. During a seven-year stint he won two league titles, two FA Cups, a League Cup and a European Cup Winners' Cup medal under boss Alex Ferguson. A strong, fearsome player, who was awesome with his back to goal, he continued to hit the target long after he left the club in 1995 and he finally hung up his boots a few days short of his 39th birthday.

Mega career highlight: Having helped Ferguson win his first trophy, the 1990 FA Cup against Crystal Palace (below), Hughes was a member of the side that reached the European Cup Winners' Cup final a year later. Ironically, the game was against his former club Barcelona and with a point to prove he netted both goals. The first was to stab home a goal-bound Steve Bruce effort, then he hit a low drive with the outside of the boot that flew in from a near impossible angle.

Name: Mark Hughes
Born: November 1, 1963
Clubs: Manchester United, Barcelona, Bayern Munich (loan), Chelsea, Southampton, Everton, Blackburn
Country: Wales
Career record: 678 games, 179 goals

THE STORY: Twice awarded the FIFA World Player of the Year, in 2004 and 2005, Ronaldinho's flicks, tricks, goals and toothy grin have helped him become the most popular and most breathtaking footballer of today. Having come to Europe in 2001, he began to make headlines in the colours of PSG, even if some of them were for his love of the Parisian nightlife rather than the football club! But that all changed when he joined Barcelona, ahead of Manchester United, in 2003 and he became an integral member of the side that won La Liga the following season. Yet it was Ronaldinho's performances in the 2005-06 season that will go down in the folklore of the club, as he almost single-handedly led Barca to Champions League glory. While he never fully fired in the final against Arsenal, his performances against Benfica and Chelsea in previous rounds helped him win the Player of the Tournament award, to sit alongside another La Liga medal and his European Footballer of the Year trophy.

Mega career highlight:
On November 19, 2005 Ronaldinho netted two great goals as Barca beat arch-rivals Real Madrid 3-0 in their own backyard. Samuel Eto'o had sent the visitors into an early lead but the game really lit up on the hour mark when Ronaldinho skipped past two challenges before racing into the box and firing past Iker Casillas. He then repeated the trick on 77 minutes, showing great pace and trickery to work an opening down the left before tucking home. The goal earned a standing ovation from the Madrid fans – a rare show of admiration not seen since Maradona played against the club.

Name: Ronaldinho
Born: March 21, 1980
Clubs: Gremio, Paris St Germain, Barcelona
Country: Brazil
Career record: 368 games, 145 goals

liverpool
STEVEN GERRARD

WAYNE'S DREAM TEAM PLAYER

Check out my DREAM TEAM on pages 58-63

WAZZA'S MENTAL CHALLENGE! 3

Test your footy knowledge with the ultimate Wazza quiz. Answers can be found on page 95

Answers can be found on page 95

ENGLAND STRIKER
PETER CROUCH

This super-tall England striker is a big favourite with the Kop. But how much do you know about him?

1 How old is he?

2 Against which team did he make his international debut?

3 How many international appearances did he make last season?

4 How many international goals did he score last season?

5 Where was he born?

6 What do he and footy England legend Kevin Keegan have in common?

1. ANSWER   2. ANSWER   3. ANSWER

4. ANSWER   5. ANSWER

6. ANSWER

GUESS THE CLUB?

Nice shirts!

This is the club's cool badge!

They are based in the most romantic city in the world.

He's a famous old boy.

The manager Paul Le Guen, used to be guvnor of Rangers!

The Parc des Princes stadium holds 48,500.

Their main striker is Portuguese.

ANSWER

SPOT THE DIFFERENCE

THERE ARE TEN DIFFERENCES BETWEEN THESE TWO PICS OF ALAN SMITH FENDING OFF JAY DEMERIT DURING THE FA CUP SEMI-FINAL. **CAN YOU SPOT THEM ALL!**

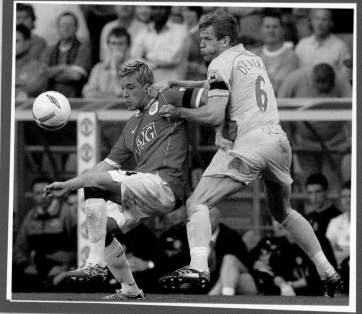

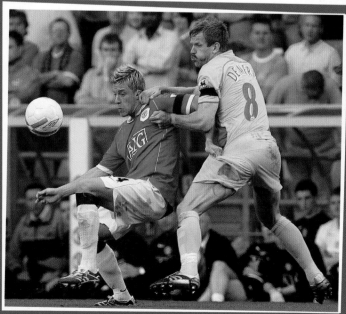

MY SCORE ..../17

35

BEAUTIFUL GAME

IT'S THE BEAUTIFUL GAME

HAVE YOU EVER

wondered what a top footy player does after training? Well, our thoroughly pooped soccer ace pops down to a local film studio to spend the afternoon dodging six-foot spiky balls and jumping over a host of other dangerous obstacles (no, not Jamie Carragher!) for a cool Coca-Cola ad. The director, Julian Gibbs, tells us how it was all done and what it was like working with Wayne 'Harrison Ford' Rooney.

WHEN YOU ARE

given the opportunity to work with a mega star like Wayne, you definitely want to do something special, so we decided to base the shoot on one of the all-time great movies – Steven Spielberg's Raiders Of The Lost Ark. We wanted to replicate the famous opening scene when archaeologist Indiana Jones has to run a booby-trapped gauntlet, complete with over-sized rolling boulder, and to bring it up to date, making it kinda harder-edged and very slick. Wayne possesses amazing power and aggression (the right sort!) and knows everything there is to know about dribbling past, outpacing, or going straight through obstacles! Straightaway, it was a brilliant match-up of idea and talent and we couldn't wait to get started…

WE WOULD BE FILMING

ten and 20-second versions of the ad. The longer cut was destined for cinema release alongside the blockbuster Spider-Man 3, and our plan was to create a hyper-real, comic book feel and look. This would mean using a process called Green Screen Action. Mega-fun and very creative! You can generate fantastic backdrops and alternative worlds, but it also meant Wayne would be acting in a room full of, well, green obstacles and enemies. He'd have to imagine what he was up against. An army of computer wizards would then add the stadium, the spiky ball, the buzzing saw and everything else you see later in the ad.

BUT NOT AS WE KNOW IT

"This is the same as training really, except the Boss doesn't shoot green balls at our heads!"

I've got lights just like these in my dining room

This ball's not velcroed to my chest, honest!

WHEN WE STARTED FILMING

I showed Wayne how to do every stunt. I told him to take it easy at first, but Wayne has only got one speed – and that's FULL ON! He did everything right first time. I suppose we shouldn't have been surprised. Wayne is a superb athlete and we all know how hard he can kick a ball, his sheer power and accuracy when shooting and his amazing agility (you shoud see the way Wayne can leap and dodge, no wonder defenders have such a hard time). Perfectionist that he is, Wayne kept saying, "Let me do it again, I can do it better!" But he was always absolutely spot on.

THIS WAS

a dream job for any director and we ended up with something quite unique. You very rarely see performances like this from a footballer and I believe Wayne could do something longer and a lot more ambitious when he's finished with footy. They'll definitely be looking for a new Harrison Ford by then and if I had my way, Wayne Rooney would have to be on the casting list!

INTRO

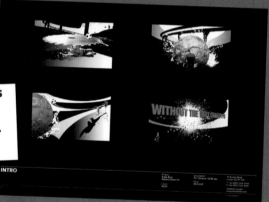

INTRO

These are the original storyboards that Coca-Cola showed Wayne when they came up with the idea. Wayne really liked it!

WITHOUT DIRTY CHALLENGES

Power and agility – Wayne's got it all

Is my trailer ready yet?!

'Fortune & glory, kid. Fortune & glory'

Wayne is going to enter the 2012 Olympics in the new discipline of the triple jump-while-balancing-a-ball-on-your-knee

BEAUTIFUL GA

MY TEAM MATES

"To win the Premiership trophy last season was, without doubt, the highlight of my career so far. The reason I joined Manchester United in the first place was because it is such a great club, with fantastic players and a brilliant manager. I therefore knew that I'd have a great chance of winning honours and while I was delighted to win the Carling Cup against Wigan in 2006, finishing top of the Premiership has been far more satisfying for me."

"With Chelsea having won successive titles with such a great squad of players, it was a great achievement to pip them to top spot by six points. It was a close-run thing in the end, with Jose Mourinho's players pushing us every step of the way, but our determination and skill saw us first over the finishing line."

"While there were some great individual performances, most notably from wing wonder Cristiano Ronaldo, our success was a real team effort with everyone in the squad playing their part. So here are the players who put Manchester United back where they belong – as champions of the Premiership!"

Profile: With United struggling for goals in the absence of the injured Louis Saha, Sir Alex Ferguson pulled off something of a masterstroke by bringing in former Celtic legend Larsson on loan from Swedish club Helsingborgs. He helped keep the forward line ticking over in the League and cup competitions, although his seven appearances in the Premiership meant he missed out on a winners' medal. United were keen to keep him for the remainder of the season but he stuck to his promise and returned home in March.

Impact rating: Six. His experience was crucial although he only chipped in with the one League goal.

APPEARANCES 5 (2) GOALS 1

DATE OF BIRTH SEPTEMBER 20, 1971

HENRIK LARSSON

YELLOW CARDS 2 RED CARDS 0

HT 5FT 9INS WT 12ST 2LBS

POSITION STRIKER

SQUAD NUMBER 17

RETURNED TO

HELSINGBORGS

Mega fact: Henrik was voted Sweden's greatest player ever in a poll conducted in 2005. He also named his son Jordan, after basketball legend Michael Jordan – Henrik's fave sportsman.

Wayne writes: "Henrik is a goalscoring legend, a great lad and was brilliant to play alongside. He brought something different to the team at just the right time and I would have loved him to stay!"

Profile: United had struggled to fill the legendary gloves of Peter Schmeichel until the big Dutchman rolled into town from Fulham in June 2005. A Champions League winner with Ajax a decade earlier, he has also played for Serie A giants Juventus and is currently skipper of the Dutch national team. At £2m, he's proved to be one of Fergie's best ever bargains and last season was his most consistent season yet in a United shirt.

Wayne writes: "Edwin has been a world class keeper for a long time now, but what impresses me most about his goalkeeping ability is his shot stopping. He has great agility."

DATE OF BIRTH OCTOBER 29, 1970

APPEARANCES 32 GOALS 0

EDWIN VAN DER SAR

YELLOW CARDS 1 RED CARDS 0

HT 6FT 5INS WT 13ST 3LBS

Impact rating: Eight. Edwin kept 12 Premiership clean sheets.

POSITION GOALKEEPER

SQUAD NUMBER 1

Mega fact: Edwin is nicknamed the Jolly Green Giant because of his height.

Profile: Having signed from Sporting Lisbon for £12.24m in 2003, Ronny just gets better and better with every passing year. Last season was easily his best yet, with his 17 Premiership goals from midfield a huge factor in United winning the Premiership. With his flicks, tricks and fearsome shooting power when cutting in from the wings, nobody was surprised when he won the PFA Player of the Year award.

Wayne writes: "Ronny's skill and pace with the ball is unbelievable, while he is really good in the air. He has added goals to his game and scored some important ones last season."

DATE OF BIRTH FEBRUARY 5, 1985

APPEARANCES 31 (3) GOALS 17

CRISTIANO RONALDO

YELLOW CARDS 2 RED CARDS 0

HT 6FT 1INS WT 12ST 2LBS

Impact rating: Ten. Ronaldo's form made him the best player in the world by a mile last season.

POSITION RIGHT MIDFIELD

SQUAD NUMBER 7

Mega fact: Ronaldo has his own clothes shop – CR7 – in his home town of Funchal.

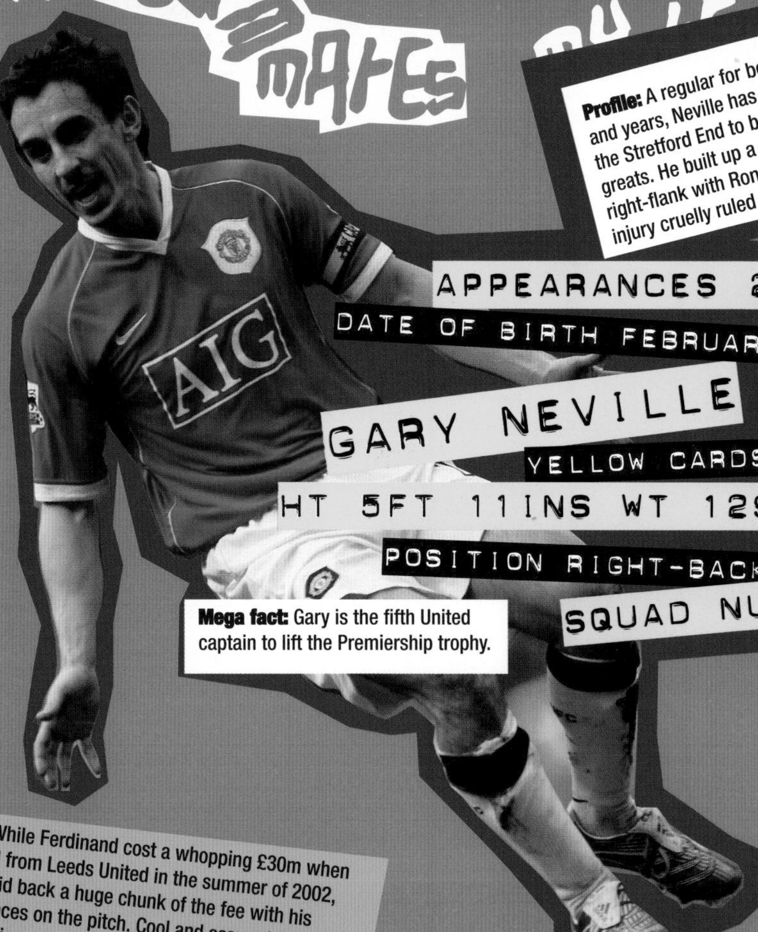

Profile: A regular for both club and country for years and years, Neville has gone from supporting United on the Stretford End to becoming one of the club's all-time greats. He built up a great partnership down United's right-flank with Ronaldo last season until an ankle injury cruelly ruled him out of the run-in to the title.

APPEARANCES 24 GOALS 0

DATE OF BIRTH FEBRUARY 18, 1975

Wayne writes: "Gary is such a determined lad. He gives everything he's got and that helps to make him such a great player. He's really influential on the pitch and in the dressing room. He's also a top moaner!"

GARY NEVILLE

YELLOW CARDS 2 RED CARDS 0

HT 5FT 11INS WT 12ST 1LB

Impact rating: Seven. As steady as ever, Neville rarely put a foot wrong. But a goal would have been nice!

POSITION RIGHT-BACK

SQUAD NUMBER 2

Mega fact: Gary is the fifth United captain to lift the Premiership trophy.

Profile: While Ferdinand cost a whopping £30m when he signed from Leeds United in the summer of 2002, he has paid back a huge chunk of the fee with his performances on the pitch. Cool and assured on the ball, his fantastic partnership with Nemanja Vidic at the heart of the United defence played a big part in the title win.

Mega fact: Ferdinand wants to make TV documentaries when he packs up playing.

RIO FERDINAND

YELLOW CARDS 2 RED CARDS 0

HT 6FT 2INS WT 13ST

Impact rating: Eight. The Prem's most consistent defender last season and one of the best behaved!

POSITION CENTRE-BACK

SQUAD NUMBER 5

APPEARANCES 33 GOALS 1

DATE OF BIRTH NOVEMBER 7, 1978

Wayne writes: "Rio is a good friend of mine at United and we'll stay close long after we stop playing football. On the pitch he is an outstanding defender, a cool customer, and his reading of the game is outstanding."

Profile: The Argentine emerged as a huge fans' favourite following his £6.9m arrival from Paris St Germain in 2004. Unfortunately, a serious knee injury kept him out of action for almost all of the 2005-06 season, losing his left-back slot to Patrice Evra in the process. Last season Heinze came back to play his part but often filled in as an emergency centre-half.

Wayne writes: "Gabby is really, really strong and very difficult to get the better of during training. He couldn't be more passionate about winning."

GABRIEL HEINZE

YELLOW CARDS 5 RED CARDS 0

HT 5FT 10INS WT 12ST 4LBS

Impact rating: Six. Steady but rarely given a chance to shine in his preferred position.

POSITION LEFT-BACK/CENTRE-BACK

SQUAD NUMBER 4

Mega fact: In 2005 Gabriel was voted best defender in the history of Paris St Germain.

APPEARANCES 17 (5) GOALS 0

DATE OF BIRTH MARCH 19, 1978

Profile: Signed from Monaco for a cool £5.5m in January 2006, Evra took a little time to settle into his new surrounds but really came good last season. A left-back who loves to get forward, he managed to keep Gabriel Heinze out of the team and was voted best left-back in the country by his Premiership peers.

Wayne writes: "Patrice is really good at going forward, which is what the modern-day full-back needs to do. He is also not bad in the air for such a small lad!"

PATRICE EVRA

DATE OF BIRTH MAY 15, 1981

APPEARANCES 22 (2) GOALS 1

YELLOW CARDS 7 RED CARDS 0

HT 5FT 8INS WT 11ST 10LB

Impact rating: Seven. Versatile Patrice helped out in left-midfield on occasions, and notched against Everton in November.

POSITION LEFT-BACK

Mega fact: Patrice put his good form of last season down to extra work in the gym.

SQUAD NUMBER 3

Profile: He's not the first-choice centre-back at United but Wes has become one of the most valued members of Sir Alex's squad. When called upon, he slots in with the minimum of fuss and has also been used at right-back or even midfield on occasions. His reward has been a fifth Premiership winners' medal.

Wayne writes: "Wes is one of those defenders who gets on quietly with his job and he does it so effectively. He is very strong in the tackle and doesn't give his marker an inch. Another big friend of mine."

DATE OF BIRTH OCTOBER 13, 1979

WES BROWN
APPEARANCES 15 (5) GOALS 0

YELLOW CARDS 3 RED CARDS 0

HT 6FT 1INS WT 13ST 2LBS

Impact rating: Six. Found it hard to displace Ferdinand and Vidic at the back.

POSITION CENTRE-BACK

SQUAD NUMBER 6

Mega fact: Brown was once called 'the most naturally gifted defender in England' by boss Sir Alex Ferguson.

Profile: Since making his £12.85m move from Fulham in 2004, Saha's Old Trafford career has been littered with injury problems. Last season was no different, as he suffered with a knee injury which ruled him out for much of the second half of the season. He still managed to score 13 goals in 25 games, in all competitions, which shows the finishing ability of the French international when he's fully fit.

Wayne writes: "Louis has been really unlucky with his injury problems. We are all hoping his troubles are now behind him because he is a top-quality finisher and a nice guy as well."

DATE OF BIRTH AUGUST 8, 1978

LOUIS SAHA
APPEARANCES 18 (6) GOALS 8

YELLOW CARDS 1 RED CARDS 0

HT 6FT 1INS WT 12ST 4LBS

Impact rating: Six. Louis had netted all his league goals by December.

POSITION STRIKER

SQUAD NUMBER 9

Mega fact: Louis had a loan spell at Newcastle United as a teenager.

Profile: A living United legend, wing-wonder Giggs made his debut as a 17-year-old in 1991 and by March 2007 had racked up his 700th appearance for the club – now leaving him tantalisingly close to breaking Sir Bobby Charlton's all-time record of 759. Despite his advancing years, he remains an awesome presence down United's left flank.

Wayne writes: "Ryan is brilliant with the ball at his feet and has great vision – which is fantastic for a striker like me. He was one of our best players last season and is a joy to play with. He is a model professional, which is the reason why he has made so many appearances for the club."

DATE OF BIRTH NOVEMBER 29, 1973

RYAN GIGGS
APPEARANCES 25 (5) GOALS 4

YELLOW CARDS 5 RED CARDS 0

HT 5FT 11INS WT 11ST

POSITION LEFT MIDFIELD

SQUAD NUMBER 11

Impact rating: Eight. Giggs still put in one of the most consistent seasons of his career – not bad for a 33-year-old!

Mega fact: Giggs is the only Premiership footballer to be mentioned in The Simpsons.

Profile: The South Korean made his name at the 2002 World Cup and, subsequently, playing in the Champions League for PSV Eindhoven. He joined United for £4m in 2005 and last season was hindered by an ankle injury, which ruled him out of action for three months. He also underwent an operation in April for a re-occurring knee problem. Nightmare!

APPEARANCES 8 (6) GOALS 5

DATE OF BIRTH FEBRUARY 25, 1981

JI-SUNG PARK

Wayne writes: "Park has suffered with injuries this season but when he plays, he is a big plus for us. He shows good movement and has a terrific engine."

YELLOW CARDS 0 RED CARDS 0

HT 5FT 8INS WT 11ST

Impact rating: Five. Hardly played but managed five goals.

POSITION LEFT MIDFIELD

SQUAD NUMBER 13

Mega fact: Before he became a footballer, Park wanted to be a PE teacher.

Profile: Having made the move from Leeds United for £7m in 2004, Smith was converted to a holding midfielder, only to suffer a broken leg and dislocated ankle against Liverpool in February 2006. He returned to the United team towards the end of last season and scored his first goal in 18 months in the 7-1 Champions League demolition of Roma.

DATE OF BIRTH OCTOBER 28, 1980

ALAN SMITH

Wayne writes: "I was delighted for Smudger when he returned to the first team because he'd worked so hard to get fit after his horrible injury. He is a really determined lad on the pitch and always works his socks off for the benefit of the team."

YELLOW CARDS 1 RED CARDS 0

HT 5FT 10INS WT 11ST 11LBS

POSITION STRIKER

APPEARANCES 6 (3) GOALS 0

SQUAD NUMBER 14

Impact rating: Four. Only featured in nine Prem games but he was still handed a winners' medal.

Mega fact: Alan was British BMX champion at the age of eight.

Profile: Vidic joined from Russian side Spartak Moscow for £7m in January 2006, and has gone from relative unknown to one of the first names on the United team-sheet. It was no coincidence that the team's form dropped when he was absent with a busted collarbone in April but he returned to play in the title-clinching victory against Manchester City.

Wayne writes: "Nemanja had a great season alongside Rio Ferdinand and is everything you want in a centre-half: really strong, competitive and great in the air. Like Smudger he is really passionate about winning."

NEMANJA VIDIC

YELLOW CARDS 7 RED CARDS 0

HT 6FT 1INS WT 13ST 2LBS

Impact rating: Nine. Formed a solid barrier with Rio Ferdinand.

POSITION CENTRE-BACK

APPEARANCES 25 GOALS 3   SQUAD NUMBER 15

DATE OF BIRTH OCTOBER 21, 1981

Mega fact: Vidic is known as 'Vida' by his team-mates.

Profile: Eyebrows were raised when United shelled out £18.6m for the Tottenham midfielder in July 2006, but he showed his quality with a storming season as United's holding player. Cool and composed on the ball, Carrick's range of passing sets him apart from many of his contemporaries and he was often the starting point for United's attacks.

Wayne writes: "Michael's passing and his vision is outstanding – he picked me out with some great balls. As the season went on, he really started to stamp his authority on the pitch and has been a great asset for the club."

Impact rating: Eight. Looked like he'd been at United for years.

MICHAEL CARRICK

YELLOW CARDS 2 RED CARDS 0

HT 6FT 1INS WT 11ST 10LBS

POSITION CENTRE MIDFIELD

DATE OF BIRTH JULY 28, 1981   SQUAD NUMBER 16

APPEARANCES 29 (4) GOALS 3

Mega fact: Michael's brother Graeme is a youth coach at Newcastle United.

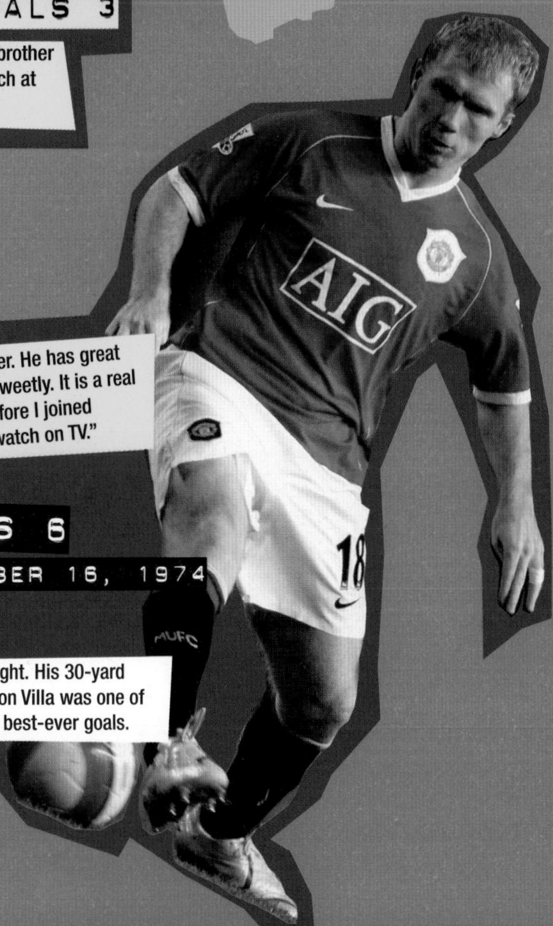

Profile: Having missed much of the previous campaign with an eye injury, Scholes stormed back to play a leading role in the club's Premiership victory – his seventh in total. With Carrick playing the holding role, Scholes was given the license to roam forward, which he did with great effect.

Wayne writes: "Paul is the ultimate midfielder. He has great passion, great vision and he hits the ball so sweetly. It is a real pleasure to play in the team with him and before I joined United, he was one of the players I loved to watch on TV."

APPEARANCES 29 (1) GOALS 6

PAUL SCHOLES   DATE OF BIRTH NOVEMBER 16, 1974

YELLOW CARDS 8 RED CARDS 1

HT 5FT 7INS WT 10ST 11LBS

Impact rating: Eight. His 30-yard volley against Aston Villa was one of the Premiership's best-ever goals.

POSITION CENTRE MIDFIELD

SQUAD NUMBER 18

Mega fact: Paul was the first England player to be sent off at Wembley, against Sweden in 1999.

45

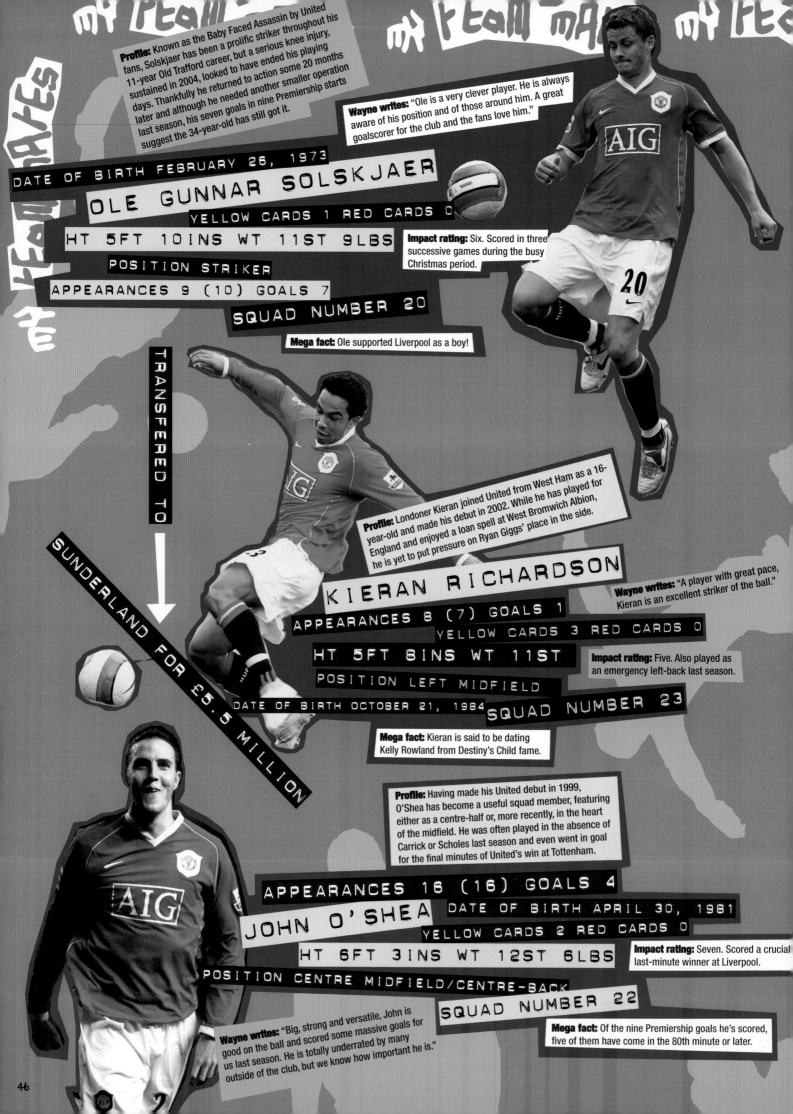

Profile: Known as the Baby Faced Assassin by United fans, Solskjaer has been a prolific striker throughout his 11-year Old Trafford career, but a serious knee injury, sustained in 2004, looked to have ended his playing days. Thankfully he returned to action some 20 months later and although he needed another smaller operation last season, his seven goals in nine Premiership starts suggest the 34-year-old has still got it.

Wayne writes: "Ole is a very clever player. He is always aware of his position and of those around him. A great goalscorer for the club and the fans love him."

DATE OF BIRTH FEBRUARY 26, 1973

OLE GUNNAR SOLSKJAER

YELLOW CARDS 1 RED CARDS 0

HT 5FT 10INS WT 11ST 9LBS

Impact rating: Six. Scored in three successive games during the busy Christmas period.

POSITION STRIKER

APPEARANCES 9 (10) GOALS 7

SQUAD NUMBER 20

Mega fact: Ole supported Liverpool as a boy!

TRANSFERED TO

SUNDERLAND FOR £5.5 MILLION

Profile: Londoner Kieran joined United from West Ham as a 16-year-old and made his debut in 2002. While he has played for England and enjoyed a loan spell at West Bromwich Albion, he is yet to put pressure on Ryan Giggs' place in the side.

KIERAN RICHARDSON

Wayne writes: "A player with great pace, Kieran is an excellent striker of the ball."

APPEARANCES 8 (7) GOALS 1

YELLOW CARDS 3 RED CARDS 0

HT 5FT 8INS WT 11ST

Impact rating: Five. Also played as an emergency left-back last season.

POSITION LEFT MIDFIELD

DATE OF BIRTH OCTOBER 21, 1984 SQUAD NUMBER 23

Mega fact: Kieran is said to be dating Kelly Rowland from Destiny's Child fame.

Profile: Having made his United debut in 1999, O'Shea has become a useful squad member, featuring either as a centre-half or, more recently, in the heart of the midfield. He was often played in the absence of Carrick or Scholes last season and even went in goal for the final minutes of United's win at Tottenham.

APPEARANCES 16 (16) GOALS 4

JOHN O'SHEA DATE OF BIRTH APRIL 30, 1981

YELLOW CARDS 2 RED CARDS 0

HT 6FT 3INS WT 12ST 6LBS

Impact rating: Seven. Scored a crucial last-minute winner at Liverpool.

POSITION CENTRE MIDFIELD/CENTRE-BACK

SQUAD NUMBER 22

Wayne writes: "Big, strong and versatile, John is good on the ball and scored some massive goals for us last season. He is totally underrated by many outside of the club, but we know how important he is."

Mega fact: Of the nine Premiership goals he's scored, five of them have come in the 80th minute or later.

Profile: The Scotland international broke into the United side in 2003 and has been a regular squad member ever since. His workmanlike performances earned him a regular starting place during the first-half of last season, and he is gradually winning over the United fans.

DATE OF BIRTH FEBRUARY 1, 1982

DARREN FLETCHER

Wayne writes: "Fletch is a player who works really hard for the team. He was vital in the big games last season and has become an important member of the squad."

YELLOW CARDS 0 RED CARDS 0

HT 6FT WT 13ST 1LB

Impact rating: Six. Scored a vital headed winner at Middlesbrough in December.

POSITION RIGHT MIDFIELD

SQUAD NUMBER 24

APPEARANCES 16 (8) GOALS 3

Mega fact: Fletcher was stopped from making his debut against Aston Villa in May 2000 because he was still on schoolboy forms.

Profile: Mikael joined United from Inter Milan in 1999 and within a couple of years had taken the left-back spot ahead of the veteran Denis Irwin. More recently he played at his favoured centre-half spot but found himself forced down the pecking order following the arrival of Nemanja Vidic. With Gabriel Heinze and Patrice Evra also battling for the left-back spot, it's been a frustrating time for the French international.

Wayne writes: "He didn't play that often last season but that was mainly because of the two injuries he's had. Mikael is still a class player though and is quick off the blocks."

MIKAEL SILVESTRE

YELLOW CARDS 0 RED CARDS 0

HT 6FT WT 12ST 7LB

Impact rating: Four. A dislocated shoulder and broken foot didn't helped his cause.

POSITION LEFT-BACK/CENTRE-HALF

DATE OF BIRTH AUGUST 9, 1977

SQUAD NUMBER 27

APPEARANCES 6 (8) GOALS 1

Mega fact: Silvestre is a close friend of Barcelona striker Thierry Henry.

Profile: The former West Bromwich Albion keeper caught the eye of Sir Alex Ferguson with a fine performance against United on the penultimate game of the 2004-05 season. One full season of Premiership goalkeeping later and he was off to United as understudy to Edwin van der Sar. Saved a penalty against Arsenal on his debut at Old Trafford and signed permanently for the club this summer.

Wayne writes: "It's important to have a really good understudy keeper and we've definitely got that in Tomasz. I found out quickly in training that he is a good shot stopper and is also really brave. He will always go in where it hurts."

APPEARANCES 6 GOALS 0

DATE OF BIRTH MARCH 23, 1982

TOMASZ KUSZCZAK

YELLOW CARDS 0 RED CARDS 0

HT 6FT 3INS WT 13ST 3LB

Impact rating: Four. Rarely featured because of van der Sar's impressive form.

POSITION GOALKEEPER

SQUAD NUMBER 29

Mega fact: In United's Carling Cup game against Crewe, his name was spelt wrong on his shirt, reading 'Zuszczak'.

47

RONALDINHO
BARCELONA

WAYNE'S DREAM TEAM PLAYER
Check out my DREAM TEAM on pages 58-63

WAZZA'S MENTAL CHALLENGE!

To finish, we have a very special competition for you!

John Terry has just scored against Brazil in the friendly at Wembley.
Wayne didn't play in the game, but he was in the stands to cheer the lads on.
Can you find eight Wazzas in the crowd?

WIN A PAIR *signed* **OF T90s**

SPOT THE WAZZA?

WAZZA 1	f 25
WAZZA 2	
WAZZA 3	
WAZZA 4	
WAZZA 5	
WAZZA 6	
WAZZA 7	
WAZZA 8	

To get you started we've found the first one. Once you have found the other seven Wazzas turn to page 95 for all the details of how to enter this super competition to win a pair of mega new T90 Laser footy boots signed by Wayne! Five runners up will each receive a copy of EA's FIFA 08.

PUT IT WHERE

These wicked new boots are the result of a special collaboration between Wayne and top Nike designer Tetsuya Tom Minami. Boffins at a top German university have discovered that nearly 70% of all shots on goal are made with the instep (that's the bit at the top of the foot) and the T90 Laser's unique design gives Wayne even more shooting accuracy. Expect to see more bulging nets this season then!

THESE BOOTS ARE MEGA AND ARE BAD NEWS FOR ALL YOU KEEPERS OUT THERE

Other players

T90 LASER

If the footy doesn't go too well, I can always get a job in a shoe shop

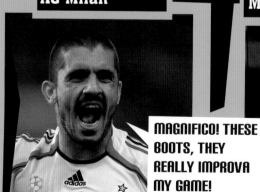

WAYNE'S TOP TEN

1

LIVERPOOL 0
MANCHESTER UNITED 1
(O'Shea 90)

When: March 3, 2007 • **Where:** Anfield
Attendance: 44,403 • **Competition:** Premiership

WAYNE SAYS: "This was a massive game, against one of our biggest rivals, and to win in the final minute was great for us. It was a result that set us up to win the title."

They say titles are won by sides who can pick up points when they're not playing well and that certainly applied to United on a sunny, Spring lunchtime at their arch rivals Liverpool. Rafa Benitez's men went close through John Arne Riise's 26th minute thunderbolt, likewise second-half efforts from Peter Crouch, Steven Gerrard and Craig Bellamy. To make matters worse for the visitors, they ended up losing Wayne through injury and then a red card for Paul Scholes. But just as the game seemed to be heading for a draw, up popped John O'Shea to slam the ball into the roof of the net after Liverpool keeper Jose Reina had dropped a clanger by spilling Cristiano Ronaldo's wicked free-kick.

2

In one of the greatest Champions League performances ever, United made a complete mockery of their first leg defeat in Rome, putting Roma to the sword with three goals in eight amazing first-half minutes. Michael Carrick curled the all-important first past stranded keeper Doni, before Alan Smith grabbed his first goal since November 2005. Wayne scored the all-important third in the 19th minute, coolly slotting home a Ryan Giggs cross, only for Cristiano Ronaldo to make it 4-0 before half-time. Another goal from the Portuguese wing wonder after the break sent Old Trafford into a frenzy while further strikes from Carrick and Patrice Evra left the Italians completely gobsmacked as they left the pitch almost in tears.

MANCHESTER UNITED 7
ROMA 1
(Carrick 12, 60, Smith 17, Rooney 19, Ronaldo 44, 49, Evra 81) – (De Rossi 69)

When: April 10, 2007 • **Where:** Old Trafford
Attendance: 74,476 • **Competition:** Champions League quarter-final, second leg

WAYNE SAYS: "This was an unbelievable result. To score seven goals against Italian opposition, who pride themselves on their defensive qualities, was a great achievement for the team. Old Trafford was completely buzzing that night."

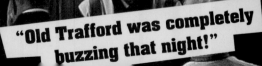
"Old Trafford was completely buzzing that night!"

3

John O'Shea took Edwin van der Sar's place and even had time to make a couple of saves

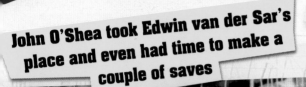

TOTTENHAM HOTSPUR 0
MANCHESTER UNITED 4

(Ronaldo 45 (p), Vidic 48, Scholes 54, Giggs 77)

When: February 4, 2007 • **Where:** White Hart Lane
Attendance: 36,146 • **Competition:** Premiership

WAYNE SAYS: "This was another difficult match for us against a very good Tottenham side, but once again we came away with a result that gave us the belief that we could go on and maintain our challenge for the Premiership title."

United broke the deadlock on the stroke of half-time when Cristiano Ronaldo scored from the spot after he was tripped by Tottenham midfielder Steed Malbranque. It was one-way traffic after the break, with Nemanja Vidic doubling United's lead with a thunderous header from ex-Spur Michael Carrick's corner. Paul Scholes then put the game out of reach, sliding in to connect with Ronaldo's top-notch cross, while Ryan Giggs completed the rout on 77 minutes when he slotted, unmarked, past Robinson. The only downer for United, who maintained a six-point lead over Chelsea, was a broken nose sustained by Edwin van der Saar, but John O'Shea took his place and even had time to make a couple of saves.

4

BOLTON WANDERERS 0
MANCHESTER UNITED 4
(Rooney 10, 16, 89, Ronaldo 82)

When: October 28, 2006 • **Where:** Reebok Stadium
Attendance: 27,229 • **Competition:** Premiership

WAYNE SAYS: "On a personal note, this was a great afternoon for me. I hadn't scored for a little while but to hit a hat–trick was the perfect response. It was nice to get the match ball signed by all the lads in the dressing room afterwards."

Wayne, without a goal in ten games, unleashed his frustrations out on Bolton to net his second hat-trick in United colours. He opened the scoring on ten minutes, latching onto Michael Carrick's pass, before burying the ball past Jussi Jaaskelainen with his left foot. It was two, six minutes later, as he curled the ball home from the edge of the box, while Cristiano Ronaldo made the game safe with eight minutes left, scoring from close range following good work from Louis Saha. But it was Rooney, four days after his 21st birthday, who stole the show and he completed his hat-trick on the stroke of full-time with a fearsome finish from midfielder Darren Fletcher's pin-point pass.

Liverpool worked their Champions League magic again as they pulled off a tremendous smash-and-grab raid in the backyard of the European Cup holders. With the likes of Messi, Ronaldinho and Deco in their ranks, Barca attacked from the off and it was no surprise when they took the lead through Deco's bullet header at the far post. The hosts messed up further chances to extend their lead and were made to pay on the stroke of half-time. Craig Bellamy connected with a Steve Finnan cross and Barca's clanger keeper Victor Valdes carried the ball over the line. The Reds doubled their account with 16 minutes remaining when Bellamy teed up John Arne Riise for a tap-in and there was even time for a late scare when Deco crashed his free-kick against a post.

BARCELONA 1
LIVERPOOL 2

5

(Deco 14) - (Bellamy 43, Riise 74)

When: February 21, 2007 • **Where:** Camp Nou
Attendance: 88,000 • **Competition:** Champions
League last 16, first leg

WAYNE SAYS: "I don't think anyone was expecting Liverpool to get a result against the current European Cup holders, especially away from home, so to score twice there and come away with the victory was a fantastic achievement by them."

VALENCIA 1
CHELSEA 2

6

(Morientes 32) – (Shevchenko 52, Essien 90)

When: April 10, 2007 • **Where:** Mestalla
Attendance: 53,000 • **Competition:** Champions
League quarter final, second leg

WAYNE SAYS: "Valencia are always a difficult team to play against, particularly when they're in front of their home fans in the Mestalla, so to score two goals and win the game shows you what Chelsea are all about."

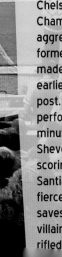

A last-minute Michael Essien goal booked Chelsea's place in the semi-finals of the Champions League, having won the tie 3-2 on aggregate. The hosts took the lead through former Liverpool striker Fernando Morientes, who made amends for hitting a post just minutes earlier by tucking home a half-volley at the far post. Chelsea needed a massive second-half performance and they set the tone just seven minutes after the re-start when striker Andrei Shevchenko finally put in a big performance, scoring from close range after Valencia keeper Santiago Canizares had parried Didier Drogba's fierce shot. Canizares had made some awesome saves that evening, but he turned from hero to villain by leaving a gap at his near post as Essien rifled home the all-important winner.

7

MANCHESTER UNITED 5 FULHAM 1

(Saha 7, Rooney 16, 64, Pearce og 15,
Ronaldo 19) – (Ferdinand og 40)

When: August 20, 2006 • Where: Old Trafford
Attendance: 75,115 • Competition: Premiership

WAYNE SAYS: "In the Premiership these days, it is so important to get off to a good start. The manager was drumming that into us before the game and so to come away with such a big win gave us plenty of confidence."

United sent out a warning to Chelsea by running riot against Fulham on the opening day of the season. With all eyes on Rooney and Ronaldo after their spat at the World Cup, the pair became brothers in arms as they totally stole the show. Louis Saha opened the scoring by taking advantage of a hapless Fulham defence, while Ian Pearce bundled the ball into his own net to make it two. Wayne then got on the act, side-footing Saha's parried effort into an empty net, before turning provider for Ronaldo, who smacked home his half-volley. Red-faced Rio Ferdinand scored an own goal before Ronny returned the favour to Rooney on 64 minutes as the final gloss was put on a pristine United performance.

It was all going wrong for United when Nemanja Vidic was carried off with a broken collarbone and Matt Derbyshire gave Blackburn a shock lead. But United showed their bottle in the second half as wave after wave of attacks were launched on Brad Friedel's goalmouth. It was only a matter of time before the visitors caved in and the equaliser arrived when Paul Scholes found some space in the box before driving the ball home. From then on there was only one outcome and three goals in 17 minutes ensured the Premiership trophy was now within touching distance.

8

MANCHESTER UNITED 4 BLACKBURN ROVERS 1

(Scholes 61, Carrick 73, Park 83, Solskjaer 90)
– (Derbyshire 29)

When: March 31, 2007 • Where: Old Trafford
Attendance: 76,098 • Competition: Premiership

WAYNE SAYS: "With Chelsea keeping the pressure on at the top, this was a vital win for us. Blackburn didn't make it easy, having gone in front, but it was important that we kept our cool. Once we'd equalised there was only one winner."

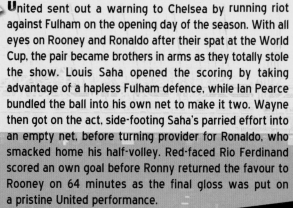

9

LIVERPOOL 3 ARSENAL 6

(Fowler 33, Gerrard 68, Hyypia 80) –
(Aliadiere 27, Baptista 40, 45, 60, 84, Song 45)

When: January 9, 2007 • **Where:** Anfield
Attendance: 42,614 • **Competition:** Carling Cup
quarter-final

WAYNE SAYS: "As was proved last season, Anfield was a tough place to get a result, so for Arsenal to score six was unbelievable. What made the achievement all the more impressive was the young side that Arsene Wenger put out that evening."

Arsenal's young guns stepped up to the plate with a stunning performance against a Liverpool side boasting six first-team regulars. Given time and space to play their flash, free-flowing football, the visitors broke the deadlock when Jeremie Aliadiere tapped home at the second attempt. Robbie Fowler equalised with his 31st League Cup goal, but from then on it was the Julio Baptista show, with the Brazilian striker showing the watching Gooners an all too rare glimpse of his undoubted talents. The highlight to his one-night-only show was a curling 25-yard free-kick for Arsenal's second, and among the glut of goals, he even had time to miss a penalty. It was the first time in nearly 77 years that Liverpool had leaked six goals at their Anfield home.

10

SHEFFIELD UNITED 1 WIGAN ATHLETIC 2

(Stead 38) – (Scharner 14, Unsworth (p) 45)
When: May 13, 2007 • **Where:** Bramall Lane
Attendance: 32,604 • **Competition:** Premiership

WAYNE SAYS: "Wigan needed a win to stay in the League, it was as simple as that. So to cope with that pressure away from home, against a team that also needed a result for the same reason, was magnificent. They showed real battling qualities on the day."

Wigan stayed up and Blades went down on a dramatic final day of the season. With West Ham also winning at champs Manchester United, Neil Warnock's side were relegated on goal difference after just one season mixing it with the big boys. Wigan struck first when defender Paul Scharner converted a Kevin Kilbane cross, but United hit back through Jon Stead – who headed home a Phil Jagielka cross while taking a battering from keeper Mike Pollitt at the same time. The visitors grabbed the all-important winner in first-half injury time when Jagielka handled a Kilbane free-kick and former Blade David Unsworth made no mistake from the spot.

WAYNE'S

As most people know, I would watch football every day if I had the chance, from the Premiership and Champions League, through to La Liga, Serie A and beyond. I just love the game of football and I particularly love watching the many world-class players that grace the beautiful game at the moment.

CA...
CLUB...
POS...

RONALDO
CLUB: Manchester United
POSITION: Midfielder

ME
CLUB: Manchester United
POSITION: Striker

MICHAEL ESSIEN
CLUB: Chelsea
POSITION: Midfielder

KAKA
CLUB: AC Milan
POSITION: Striker

"I have had the pleasure of playing alongside or against most of the players selected and each one ex...

With such an abundance of talent about, it was really tricky picking my Dream Team and there are players who have ended up on my subs' bench who would not have looked out of place in the starting eleven. But I have made my choice from the players who have really stood out for their clubs in the past year, both domestically and in the Champions League.

ON DA BENCH

IKER CASILLAS
CLUB: Real Madrid
POSITION: Goalkeeper

JOHN TERRY
CLUB: Chelea
POSITION: Defender

OWEN HARGREAVES
CLUB: Manchester United
POSITION: Midfielder

THIERRY HENRY
CLUB: Barcelona
POSITION: Striker

DREAM TEAM

PETR CECH
CLUB: *Chelsea*
POSITION: *Goalkeeper*

ALESSANDRO NESTA
CLUB: *AC Milan*
POSITION: *Centre-back*

ILLE
er United
ht-back

RIO FERDINAND
CLUB: *Manchester United*
POSITION: *Centre-back*

PAOLO MALDINI
CLUB: *AC Milan*
POSITION: *Left-back*

STEVEN GERRARD
CLUB: *Liverpool*
POSITION: *Midfielder*

RONALDINHO
CLUB: *Barcelona*
POSITION: *Midfielder*

their own chosen position. Playing 4-4-2, it's an attack-minded line-up and one which would look to excite the crowd at every opportunity"

"I'VE SELECTED A TEAM WITH FLAIR, A TEAM WITH PRIDE, A TEAM WITH PASSION. BUT MOST OF ALL I'VE SELECTED A TEAM OF WINNERS. TAKE US ON AT YOUR PERIL!"

NOW TURN OVER TO FIND OUT WHY ROONEY PICKED WHO HE DID...

WAYNE'S DREAM TEAM

Petr Cech – Goalkeeper

Club: Chelsea

COUNTRY: Czech Republic

Age: 25

Career appearances: 257

Career goals: 0

Widely regarded as the best keeper in the world, Cech is described by Chelsea boss Jose Mourinho as one of his 'untouchables'. Proof of his immense presence came last season when he fractured his skull against Reading and was sidelined for three months. In his absence, the Chelsea back-four looked all at sea, and the poor run of results at the time ultimately cost Blues the chance of a third successive Premiership victory.

WAYNE SAYS: "When you're bearing down on goal against Chelsea, Petr has such a presence that it looks as if he's filled the entire goal! He is a great shot stopper, is very agile considering his height and instils great confidence in the players around him. Like our own Edwin van der Sar at United, he wins games on his own with some of the saves he pulls off."

Gary Neville – Right-back

Club: Manchester United

Country: England

Age: 32

Career appearances: 449

Career goals: 5

A regular for club and country for more than 12 years, Gary is one of the most consistent players ever to grace the Premiership and has the medals in his locker to back up his talent: seven Premiership, one Champions League and three FA Cup medals is the haul so far. A full-back who loves to get forward, Neville has a great understanding down Man United's right flank with Cristiano Ronaldo and despite his advancing years, shows no sign of slowing up.

WAYNE SAYS: "As one of the more experienced members of the United side, Gary commands great respect from his team-mates but he is also a great lad to have around the dressing room with his humour and leadership qualities. On the pitch there is no better full-back around and I really felt for him when he missed the run-in to last season with his ankle injury."

"ON THE PITCH THERE IS NO BETTER FULL-BACK AROUND!"

WAYNE'S DREAM

"THE WORD LEGEND IS USED TOO EASILY IN FOOTBALL, BUT IT REALLY DOES APPLY WHEN TALKING ABOUT MALDINI"

Paolo Maldini - Left-back

Club: AC Milan
Country: Italy
Age: 39
Career appearances: 726
Career goals: 35

Regarded as the best defender of his era, Maldini will go down as a true legend of Italian football... once he finally packs up playing! A record 126 caps for Italy, seven Serie A titles and five European Cup wins, Paolo showed no signs of letting up last season when he led Milan - his only club - to glory in the Champions League final against Liverpool. While his legs might have slowed down, there are few better at reading the game.

WAYNE SAYS: "The word legend is used too easily in football, but it really does apply when talking about Maldini. To have performed at the highest level for as long as he has says so much for his ability and character as a footballer. While he only played for 45 minutes against us in the Champions League last season, he showed he is still as good as ever with his top display in the final against Liverpool."

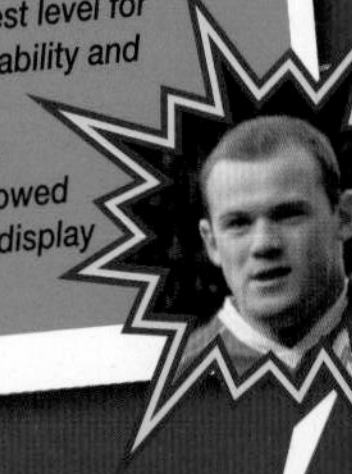

Rio Ferdinand - Centre-back

Club: Manchester United
Country: England
Age: 28
Career appearances: 399
Career goals: 9

One of the Premiership's most accomplished defenders, Rio's calmness on the ball stems from his early days at West Ham when he used to play at the heart of midfield. A good reader of the game, his partnership with Nemanja Vidic was one of the main reasons why Manchester United won the League last season. His £30m fee was mega at the time, but in the five years since his transfer from Leeds United, Rio has more than paid back United with his performances. Also a top man for England.

WAYNE SAYS: "When United play out from the back, Rio's more than happy to have the ball because he is so comfortable with it. He's a defender you can really rely on in the big games and is one of the most consistent performers at the club. Off the pitch, Rio is a great guy, the life and soul of the party."

Alessandro Nesta - Centre-back

Club: AC Milan
Country: Italy
Age: 31
Career appearances: 399
Career goals: 3

With fantastic technical ability, rapid speed and a real ruggedness in the tackle, Nesta is regarded by many as the best centre-back in world football. Having made his name at Lazio, his career really took off following a move to Milan in 2002, winning the Champions League in his first season at the San Siro. Since then it has been success all the way, winning the Scudetto in 2004, the World Cup with Italy in 2006 and the Champions League, with victory against Rafa's boys, last season.

WAYNE SAYS: "A truly accomplished defender who has been at the top of his profession for a long, long time. Apart from his obvious strengths on the ball, Nesta has great positional sense, which really sets him apart from other top-class defenders. He is a leader of his back-line, in a similar way to John Terry at Chelsea."

Michael Essien - Midfielder

Club: Chelsea

Country: Ghana

Age: 24

Career appearances: 222

Career goals: 31

Essien emerged as Chelsea's Player of the Year last season, which is no mean feat given the sprinkling of superstars in their squad. A robust midfielder who likes to break up play for the more attack-minded individuals in the side, Essien also performed admirably as an emergency defender last season and is now one of the first names on the team sheet for Jose Mourinho. He also has a mean shot on him - just ask Arsenal keeper Jens Lehmann who saw a 25-yard shot whistle past him at The Bridge last December.

WAYNE SAYS: "A fierce competitor, Michael is everything you want from a midfielder. He has a tremendous engine, a good range of passing and is very precise with that passing. If that wasn't enough, he does himself justice every time he plays at the back in the absence of either John Terry or Ricardo Carvalho. Versatile players like that are invaluable."

Cristiano Ronaldo - Midfielder

Club: Manchester United

Country: Portugal

Age: 22

Career appearances: 203

Career goals: 55

With 20 goals to his name from midfield, Ronaldo was head and shoulders above every other player in the Premiership last season and fully deserving of his PFA Player of the Year trophy. He's always had the skills to pay the bills, but Ronny added consistency and goals to his game to emerge as one of the most exciting players ever seen. He was the difference as United pipped Chelsea to the title and his reward was a bumper new contract, which pleased the Old Trafford fans who feared he could be heading to La Liga.

WAYNE SAYS: "Ronny was deserving of all the accolades that came his way last season. When he's in full flow, he is a nightmare to defend against but what sets him apart from most wide players is the fact that he backs up his wing play with plenty of goals. He is a player who gets the fans up off their seats and I'm delighted that he's committed his future to United. And the frightening thing is that he can only get better."

Steven Gerrard - Midfielder

Club: Liverpool

Country: England

Age: 27

Career appearances: 324

Career goals: 56

A player that would walk into any team in the world, Stevie G is the ultimate midfielder. Strong in the tackle, a crisp passer of the ball and with an awesome shot, he strikes fear into opponents whenever he steps onto the pitch. Gerrard proved his worth again last season, leading Liverpool to the final of the Champions League against AC Milan, and while the Reds came away on the wrong end of a 2-1 scoreline, Gerrard could be proud of his own performance.

WAYNE SAYS: "Stevie just gets better and better with every passing season. When he steps onto the pitch, you know exactly what you are going to get from him and he inspires the players around him. A true leader of men, I really enjoy linking up with him when I'm on England duty and as a fellow Scouser we always have plenty of banter together. He is a nice guy off the pitch, too, and a popular team-mate."

"HE IS ALREADY ONE OR TWO STEPS AHEAD OF HIS MARKER AND CAN DRIFT ALL OVER THE PITCH!"

Kaka - Striker

Club: AC Milan

Country: Brazil

Age: 25

Career appearances: 239

Career goals: 93

While Kaka's talents have long been recognised, the Brazilian really came to the fore at AC Milan following Andrei Shevchenko's departure to Chelsea last summer. From that moment on, he became the focal point of the team's attack and it was no surprise to see him emerge as the Champions League's stand-out player as Milan won the cherished trophy. Following the win, Pele said he was the world's best player and may turn out to be the best the game has ever seen in the coming seasons. Nuff said!

WAYNE SAYS: "Having seen Kaka in close quarters in last season's Champions League, he has tremendous speed of thought and that can be the difference at the very highest level. He is already one or two steps ahead of his marker and can drift all over the pitch, making him very difficult to pick up. Add his undoubted skill and eye for goal to the mix, then you have a very special player indeed."

Ronaldinho - Midfielder

Club: Barcelona

Country: Brazil

Age: 27

Career appearances: 367

Career goals: 144

Arguably the most gifted player on the planet, Ronaldinho's skills - particularly when he's under pressure from opposing players - is simply breathtaking. The Brazilian is rarely seen without a big smile on his face and was instrumental in Barcelona's Champions League and La Liga double in 2006. He would have taken last season's early exit from the Champions League and Real Madrid's last-day championship victory personally, so you can expect him to come out with all guns blazing this year.

WAYNE SAYS: "I had the chance to meet Ronaldinho personally when we did a TV ad for the FIFA 06 computer game and just to watch him perform his tricks was great. But to then do those same tricks in an actual match situation shows what a special talent he is. I know only too well that it can be difficult when you're being tightly marked by an opposing defender but nine times out of ten Ronaldinho will leave his marker red faced with one outrageous moment of skill. One of the best players of his generation."

THIS IS THE DREAM TEAM I'VE CHOSEN. LET THE FUN BEGIN!

MATCH DAY

11.30

"When we're at home for a three o'clock kick-off, we have to be at Old Trafford at least three hours before the start. I've just arrived in the players' car park."

Wayne drives himself to the ground. Unlike on a training day, when he has to be at the Carrington traning complex by nine, he can have a nice lie-in!

It's May 13 2007, t' of the Prem seaso heads into Old Tra match against We Manchester Unite champions and th medals will be pr the game. For the top-flight surviva

11.31

Give it a good wax and a polish, please mate!

"I don't have to worry about parking my car because the match-day security guys do that for me and all the other United players."

Footy players and their cars! Wazza's other motors include an Audi and a Lamborghini!

WITH WAYNE

11.33

It's quickly off to the United dressing room where Wazza starts to prepare!

Does anybody know where the changing rooms are?

...st day
...d Wayne
... for the
...am.
... already
...phy and
...ted after
...mmers,
...till at stake.

"The first thing I do when I get inside Old Trafford is say 'hello' to the guys who are always at the entrance. Then I drop my wash bag off in the changing room."

11.35

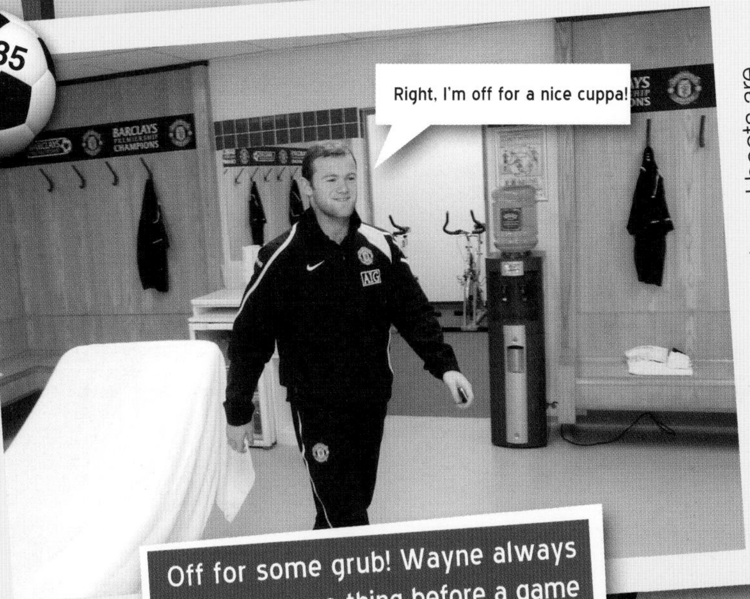

Right, I'm off for a nice cuppa!

Off for some grub! Wayne always eats the same thing before a game – spaghetti bolognese and a piece of chicken. No pudding though!

"After I've checked my kit and boots are all fine, and I've had a bit of a laugh with Albert our kit man, I go for a cup of tea."

"When we're at home for a three o'clock kick-off, we have to be at Old Trafford at least three hours before the start. I've just arrived in the player's car park"

11.45

Come on, Choccy every time!

"Once my match-day gear is all checked, I go through to the lounge for that cup of tea and some banter with the coaches. Then we sit down together for our pre-match meal."

It's straight to the biscuit tin for Wayne. Choccy or jammie dodger?

13.45

According to Curbs, West Ham are playing that Tevez dude up front, in midfield, in defence and in goal!

The players' lounge is strictly off-limits to family and friends until after the match.

14.00

"In the changing room, I'm here on the physio couch, waiting for the boss to come in and go through any last minute changes and the team."

It's time to get serious as the players head back into the changing room

"The best moment in football for me – running out onto the pitch at three o'clock, four o'clock or any other kick-off times during the course of the season"

14.10

Are you sure we're playing at home today, Ronny? Give the Boss a call, and tell him we're here!

"Not long to kick off now. Me and Ronny are planning one last prank... just to ease any pre-match tension there might be!"

Apparently Cristiano Ronaldo is the biggest joker in the changing room and plays tricks on his team-mates. Good job he does so well on the pitch then!

"In the players' lounge we all sit down and watch videos of the opposition's set-pieces and we get our own personal briefings."

14.57

The last day of the season and champions United are given a Guard of Honour!

"The best moment in football for me – running out onto the pitch at three o'clock, four o'clock or any other kick-off times during the course of the season."

15.05

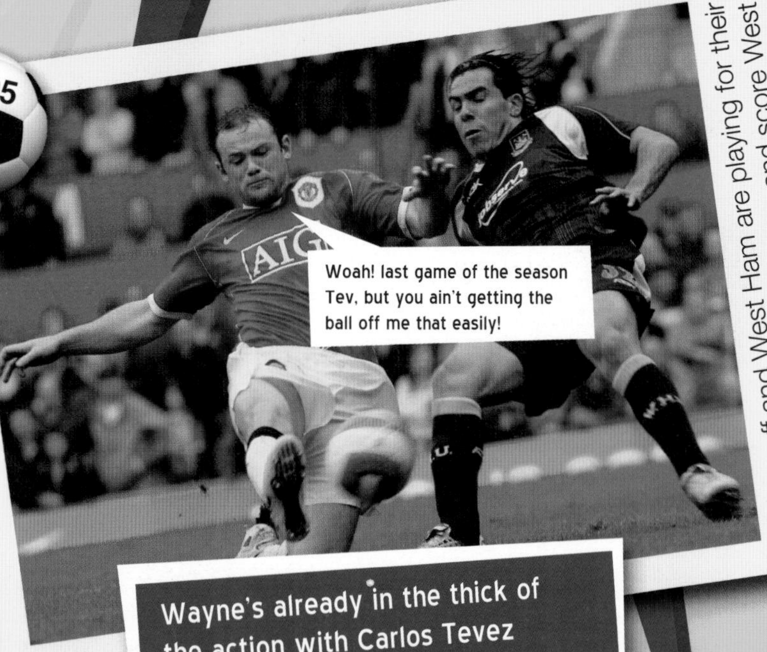

Woah! last game of the season Tev, but you ain't getting the ball off me that easily!

"We're off and West Ham are playing for their lives. Carlos Tevez will go on and score West Ham's vital relegation-avoiding goal on the stroke of half time. Shame that we didn't win."

Wayne's already in the thick of the action with Carlos Tevez

17.15

CHAMPIONS
16

17.00

"It was not the result we wanted but while West Ham celebrated, we had some celebrating of our own to do by lifting the Premiership trophy!"

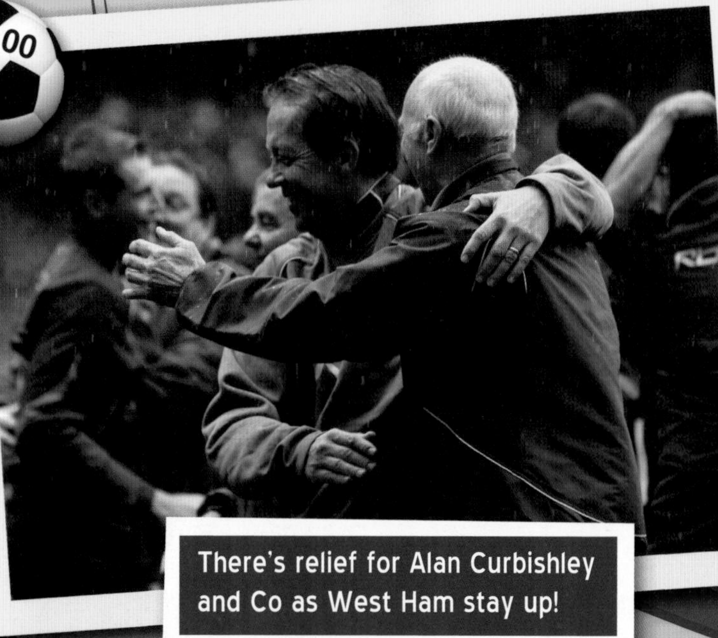

There's relief for Alan Curbishley and Co as West Ham stay up!

17.10

"We couldn't have done it without the support of our brilliant fans."

"Champions! Champions!"

"The Stretford End fans hold up posters celebrating the club's 16th League title!"

Says it all, really

17.35

Let the party begin! Wayne and his United team-mates pop open the champers to toast their title success!

"Of course we knew we had won the Prem before the kick-off, so the champagne was already on ice in the changing room!"

WAZZA'S WICKED FIVE-A-SIDE

After playing in Nike's new FIVE-A-SIDE tournament, I have come up with three wicked

WAYNE'S TOP 3 FIVE-A-SIDE TIPS

1 USE THE BOARDS FOR A REBOUND PASS

When you're playing indoors you can use the boards for a rebound pass. As a defender runs towards you, knock the ball into the boards, run past the defender, and collect the ball as it rebounds back. Practise this and it will feel like you have a sixth man on your team.

WAZZA
AGE: 21
CLUB: Manchester United
POSITION: Striker
SKILLS: With a fantastic eye for goal. Wayne has awesome shooting ability. guaranteeing goals galore.

WAZZA
AGE: 21
CLUB: Manchester United
POSITION: Goalie
SKILLS: On the training pitch you can't keep Wazza out of goal where he's a great shot stopper.

WAZZA
AGE: 21
CLUB: Manchester United
POSITION: Defender
SKILLS: The hard-man of the five-a-side pitch. Wayne has all the tackling qualities to stop his opponents stone dead in their tracks.

ZZA
1
Manchester United
ON: Winger
S: With shear pace and the power to ghost ponents. Wayne would supply loads of mega sses for the easiest of goals.

WAZZA
AGE: 21
CLUB: Manchester United
POSITION: Midfielder
SKILLS: With excellent stamina to last the pace and great close control. Wayne will go past the opposition

tips **and the team I'd love to play against!**

2 THE FEINT AND SHOOT

You know when Ronaldinho does his tricky thing of looking one way and passing the ball the other? Well, you can do the same sort of thing in front of goal. During a break-away, turn to the far side of the goal just for an instant then turn back and shoot. The goalie will almost always follow your first move and the goal will open up for a less obstructed shot. When you get this right you can make the keeper feel silly like Portsmouth's David James did at Old Trafford when I chipped him from outside the box, during our FA Cup fourth round victory – tee hee!

3 THE TIGHT TURN AND PASS

If you are running with the ball and a defender is keeping pace with you, try turning in a tight circle away from him in the opposite direction. So if the defender is right up on your shoulder, say on the left, turn right as tightly as possible. Chances are the defender will run past you and then try to follow by going around your back. It will give you those vital extra seconds to make that killer pass or get your shot away.

KAKA
AGE: 25
CLUB: AC Milan
POSITION: Striker
SKILLS: With the ball at his feet, Kaka can make time for himself with one drop of the shoulder, while he is also fantastic at losing his marker and running into space to pick up a pass from his team-mates. Both these skills are vital in the confined spaces of a five-a-side pitch. He also knows exactly where the goal is.

GERRARD
AGE: 27
CLUB: Liverpool
POSITION: Defensive Midfielder/Rush keeper!
SKILLS: Tackling, like in the 11-a-side game, remains a key element and that's where Stevie fits in. He can use his no-nonsense style to hustle and bustle opponents off the ball. With his awesome shooting power, Gerrard would have no problem finding the target. I'd also fancy him as their keeper!

ZIDANE
AGE: 35
CLUB: Retired (boo hoo!)
POSITION: Midfielder
SKILLS: As the ultimate midfielder in his playing days, Zidane has a sprinkling of everything. From skills on the ball and an eye for a pass, through to his shooting and tracking back to defend, Zizou can do it all. He would be the talisman of the team, working the middle area of the pitch and always keeping the ball moving forward.

RONALDINHO
AGE: 27
CLUB: Barcelona
POSITION: Midfielder
SKILLS: There iss always room for flamboyancy in the five-a-side arena and who better than Ronaldinho to provide the flicks and tricks which often make the difference at this level? When there is little room to move, Ronny's breathtaking tricks can put his marker into a daze, while sending a team-mate free to score in the process.

RONALDO
AGE: 22
CLUB: Manchester United
POSITION: Winger/Striker
SKILLS: Cristiano is up there with the best of them when it comes to skills, and his step-overs would be fantastic to watch on a five-a-side pitch. Those quick feet would mesmerise opponents. From this team, he would be the man to put the ball in the net more than any other. An awesome striker of the ball.

MANCHESTER UNITED'S MAGICAL SEASON

FA PREMIERSHIP

MATCH-BY-MATCH GUIDE OF HOW MANCHESTER UNITED WON THE 2006-07 FA PREMIERSHIP TITLE

Before the start of the season you have the usual thoughts: will this be our year? How will I play? How will things go? The Boss told us how vital it was to get off to a good start in the Prem and not let Chelsea get ahead of us in the same way they had in previous seasons. I was a bit worried about how we were going to replace Ruud van Nistelrooy's goals, but Paul Scholes was coming back and we'd bought Michael Carrick from Tottenham who I felt could add another dimension to our game. In the end, **we were Magic!**

As for me? My early-season form wasn't as consistent as it should have been. I did give the ball away sometimes when I shouldn't have done, didn't always finish when I was one-on-one with the goalie. Playing different positions perhaps didn't help, sometimes out left, sometimes behind the striker, sometimes as the main striker.

I think as I've got older – I'm all of 21 now! – I do try to think about the game more, I try to be more sensible. I now realise it's better to cut out two defenders with a pass rather than dribble past them. I'm also more aware when people are in a better position, so I'll pass to them rather than be greedy. I like to think my assists have been the best at the club, laying goals on for others, setting up vital moves.

Once the season was over, we could reflect on a job well done. Our Premiership season couldn't have gone any better and we reached the semi-finals of the Champions League. We were very unlucky to lose the FA Cup final to Chelsea – my runners-up medal is still in my washbag – but I look at my Premiership medal all the time. I scored 24 goals, which was better than the previous season, so once again I kept up my self-imposed target of getting more goals in every season I play.

Next season I hope we'll do even better and, of course we'll have new star players in the squad to shine, including Owen Hargreaves who I know from the England set up. He'll be a big positive. I've now had five seasons in the Premiership and I feel like I've become a senior player for the club. But when the new season starts, I felt just like a big kid again. But for now let's look back on what was a magic season for Manchester United!

"A FANTASTIC START! WE ALL HOPED THIS WOULD SET THE TONE FOR THE REST OF THE SEASON"

1 | MANCHESTER UNITED 5 / FULHAM 1

FA PREMIERSHIP

DATE: Sunday, August 20

ATTENDANCE: 75,115 (Old Trafford)

REFEREE: Andre Marriner

GOALS: 7 MINS (1-0) SAHA - Louis Saha scored with a glancing header from a Ryan Giggs cross; **14 MINS (2-0) PEARCE OWN GOAL** – Giggs threaded a superb pass through the Fulham defence to find Wayne Rooney, who in turn played a pass to Cristiano Ronaldo. He fed Saha, who sent a low cross over that was intercepted and inadvertently directed into his own net by Fulham's Ian Pearce; **15 MINS (3-0) ROONEY** - a tap-in for Rooney after goalkeeper Antii Niemi parried Saha's volley at the far post from Paul Scholes and Gary Neville's quickly-worked free kick; **18 MINS (4-0) RONALDO** - volleyed past the unprotected goalkeeper Niemi after Franck Queudrue completely missed an attempted clearance of Rooney's floated cross-field pass; **39 MINS (4-1) FERDINAND OWN GOAL** – Heidar Helguson's shot took a severe deflection off Rio Ferdinand and looped over the stranded Edwin van der Sar; **63 MINS (5-1) ROONEY** - a superb move down the right ended with a Wes Brown cross that Rooney fired in.

THE GAME: Manchester United made a stunning start to the new season with a superlative performance. Rooney recovered from a groin injury to score twice and give a Man-of-the-Match performance. Any World Cup differences he may have had with Ronaldo, who had to endure boos and jeers every time he touched the ball from visiting fans, no longer existed as the two played an integral part in a devastating onslaught that had Fulham 4-0 down by the 18th minute. United showed some brilliant one-touch play.

SIR ALEX FERGUSON: "We explained to him [Ronaldo] what had happened to David Beckham. We told him that it would be another seven-day wonder. He's got nerve to handle it."

WAYNE ROONEY: "People who don't know us have said a lot about us this summer but we let our football do the talking today."

MANCHESTER UTD	FULHAM
Van der Sar	Niemi
Neville	Rosenior
Subbed HT (Silvestre)	Christanval
Ferdinand OG	Pearce OG
Brown	Queudrue
Evra	Brown
Ronaldo ☺	*Subbed 61 mins (Radzinski)*
O'Shea	Diop
Scholes	Bullard
Giggs	Boa Morte
Subbed 61 mins (Park)	John
Rooney ☺☺	*Subbed 64 mins (McBride)*
Saha	Helguson
Subbed 61 mins (Solskjaer)	*sub: Radzinski*
sub: Silvestre	*sub: McBride*
sub: Park	**Subs not used:** *Crossley, Volz, Bocanegra.*
sub: Solskjaer	**Coach:** *Chris Coleman*
Subs not used: *Fletcher, Kuszczak.*	
Coach: *Sir Alex Ferguson*	

12 MINS (0-1) SILVESTRE - Giggs BROUGHT THE BALL FORWARD BEFORE PASSING TO SAHA WHO PICKED OUT THE OVERLAPPING SILVESTRE ON THE LEFT. SILVESTRE CUT INSIDE THEN DRILLED A LOW SHOT PAST GOALKEEPER RICHARD LEE AND INTO THE FAR CORNER OF THE NET!

82 MINS (2-0) SAHA - AFTER CHASING A WES BROWN CROSS, SAHA TURNED GOAL-WARD AND SHOT PAST CARSON FROM JUST OUTSIDE THE PENALTY AREA!

WATFORD	MANCHESTER UTD
Lee	Van der Sar
Doyley	Brown
DeMerit	Silvestre ⚽
Shittu	Ferdinand
Powell	O'Shea
Young	Ronaldo
Mahon	Fletcher
Subbed 75 mins (Bangura)	Carrick
Bouazza	Subbed 75 mins (Richardson)
Subbed 31 mins (Spring)	Giggs ⚽
King	Saha
Henderson	Solskjaer
Francis ⚽	Subbed 59 mins (Park)
Subbed 65 mins (Stewart)	sub: Richardson
sub: Bangura ⚽	sub: Park
sub: Spring	Subs not used: Kuszczak, Evra, Rossi
Subs not used: Chamberlain, Mackay	Coach: Sir Alex Ferguson
Coach: Adrian Boothroyd	

3 WATFORD 1 MANCHESTER UNITED 2

FA PREMIERSHIP

DATE: Saturday August 26

ATTENDANCE: 19,453 (Vicarage Road Stadium)

REFEREE: Phil Dowd

GOALS: 12 MINS (0-1) SILVESTRE - Giggs brought the ball forward before passing to Saha, who picked out the overlapping Mikael Silvestre on the left. Silvestre cut inside then drilled a low shot past goalkeeper Richard Lee and into the far corner of the net; 34 MINS (1-1) FRANCIS - Silvestre was beaten by a dummy from Ashley Young before hitting a low cross which Ferdinand failed to cut out leaving the unmarked Damien Francis to equalise; 52 MINS (1-2) GIGGS - Matthew Spring's pass back intended for Lee was intercepted by Giggs who broke into the area, rounded the keeper, before turning the ball home for the visitors.

THE GAME: Solskjaer made his first start for two years following knee surgery, while £18.6 million summer signing Michael Carrick also made his first Premiership start for United. In contrast, the veteran Giggs was making his 600th appearance for the club and his match-winning goal against newly-promoted Watford made him the eighth different player to score for United in their first three Premiership games. It was not the best performance by Ferguson's Premiership frontrunners, but they got the result. Watford goalkeeper Lee was only playing because Hornets first choice Ben Foster was on loan at Vicarage Road from Old Trafford, and was therefore not allowed to play in the game.

SIR ALEX FERGUSON: "When we counter-attacked we should have passed the ball better. We're normally good at this but that quality deserted us in these moments."

2 CHARLTON ATHLETIC 0 MANCHESTER UNITED 3

FA PREMIERSHIP

DATE: Wednesday August 23

ATTENDANCE: 25,422 (The Valley)

REFEREE: Chris Foy

GOALS: 46 MINS (1-0) FLETCHER - defender Jon Fortune failed to clear Ji-Sung Park's low centre and Darren Fletcher seized possession, held off two challenges and carved out the space to shoot home; 82 MINS (2-0) SAHA - after chasing a Wes Brown cross, Saha turned goal-ward and shot past Scott Carson from just outside the penalty area; 90 MINS (3-0) SOLSKJAER - netted with a tap in from a cut-back by Saha.

THE GAME: United were the only Premiership team to win their opening two fixtures after this 3-0 win at The Valley. It was an easy victory achieved without Rooney and Scholes – both suspended for being sent-off in the pre-season LG Amsterdam Tournament – and it could've been by a wider margin. In addition to goals from Fletcher, Saha and Ole Gunnar Solskjaer (his first for United since September 2003) United also hit the woodwork three times through Giggs, Ronaldo (booed but played superbly) and Park.

SIR ALEX FERGUSON [ON SOLSKJAER'S GOAL]: "That was a great moment. You see a player persevere through a torrid time that he had for two years with his injury and never lose faith. He got his repayment tonight."

CHARLTON ATHLETIC	MANCHESTER UTD
Carson	Van der Sar
Young	Brown
El Karkouri	Ferdinand
Fortune	Silvestre
Hreidarsson	Evra
Hughes	Fletcher ⚽
Holland	Park
Faye	Subbed 77 mins (Carrick)
Subbed 82 mins (Rommedahl)	O'Shea
Ambrose	Giggs
Hasselbaink	Subbed 82 mins (Solskjaer)
Subbed 65 mins (M Bent)	Saha ⚽
D Bent	Ronaldo
sub: Rommedahl	sub: Carrick
sub: M Bent	sub: Solskjaer ⚽
Subs not used: Myhre, Kishishev, Lisbie	Subs not used: Kuszczak, Rossi, Richardson
Coach: Iain Dowie	Coach: Sir Alex Ferguson

4 MANCHESTER UNITED 1 TOTTENHAM HOTSPUR 0

FA PREMIERSHIP

DATE: Saturday September 9

ATTENDANCE: 75,453 (Old Trafford)

REFEREE: Mike Riley

GOAL: 9 MINS (1-0) GIGGS - Tottenham inexplicably failed to form a defensive wall allowing Ronaldo a direct shot on goal from his free kick. Goalkeeper Paul Robinson parried the effort but Giggs was on hand to follow up and head home via the underside of the crossbar.

THE GAME: United were temporarily knocked off the top of the table for a few hours, due to their late kick-off, although returning to pole position wasn't straight forward before the biggest crowd ever to see a Premiership match. Tottenham dominated for long periods but lacked the penetrative power to find the net. United, for their part, found many of their attempts at attack snuffed out before any significant danger was created. Giggs – who picked up his Barclays Premiership Player of the Month for August before the game – was playing the Rooney role alongside Saha, and got the only goal of the game early on. The narrow victory maintained United's 100 per cent start to their Premiership campaign.

SIR ALEX FERGUSON ON RYAN GIGGS: "He's been fantastic for this club, there's no question of that. He's using his experience and maturity now, which is very pleasing because we need people who can do that."

MANCHESTER UTD	TOTTENHAM HOTSPUR
Van der Sar	Robinson
Neville	Chimbonda
Ferdinand	Dawson
Brown	King
Evra	Subbed 81 mins (Murphy)
Ronaldo	Assou-Ekotto
Subbed 90 mins (Silvestre)	Jenas
Carrick	Zokora
Subbed 79 mins (Fletcher)	Davids
O'Shea	Subbed 57 mins (Ziegler)
Richardson	Ghaly
Subbed 70 mins (Park)	Keane
Giggs ⚽	Subbed 57 mins (Defoe)
Saha	Mido
sub: Silvestre	sub: Murphy
sub: Fletcher	sub: Ziegler
sub: Park	sub: Defoe
Subs not used: Kuszczak, Solskjaer	Subs not used: Cerny, Huddlestone
Coach: Sir Alex Ferguson	Coach: Martin Jol

"I WAS SUSPENDED SO I WATCHED THE LADS IN AN ENGLISH PUB IN DUBAI WITH A BUNCH OF CHELSEA FANS!"

5 MANCHESTER UNITED 0
ARSENAL 1

FA PREMIERSHIP

DATE: Sunday September 17

ATTENDANCE: 75,595 (Old Trafford)

REFEREE: Graham Poll

GOAL: 86 MINS (0-1) ADEBAYOR - Cesc Fabregas won the ball from Ronaldo and headed goalward before playing a perfectly-timed and paced pass for Emmanuel Adebayor to fire his shot underneath the diving Tomasz Kuszczak.

THE GAME: Wayne Rooney and Paul Scholes returned to Premiership action after serving their suspensions and found themselves in a team outplayed by Arsenal. The Gunners showed excellent movement and imagination, unlike United who were below their best. United goalkeeper Kuszczak, making his debut as Van der Sar was ruled out with a stomach bug, saved a Gilberto Silva penalty and also kept the Arsenal attack at bay with a couple more saves to deny Adebayor and Tomas Rosicky. It looked like United had gained a point until Adebayor's late goal earned the Gunners their first win of the season. Coupled with this defeat was 10-man's Chelsea's home win over Liverpool which meant United were on level points with their main rivals for the title – and a point behind shock new Premiership leaders Portsmouth!

SIR ALEX FERGUSON: "I don't think it was a bad performance but I was disappointed by our tiredness in the second-half. I think the pace and emotion of the Celtic game, which was played in a real Scotland v England tempo, might have affected us."

WAYNE ROONEY: "One result that stands out in my mind is losing to Arsenal at home in September. We went on a brilliant run of wins after that... that's one of the best things about this team; we're defiant after a defeat."

MANCHESTER UTD	ARSENAL
Kuszczak	Lehmann
Neville	Eboue
Ferdinand	Djourou
Brown	Toure
Silvestre	Gallas
Subbed 23 mins (Evra)	Rosicky
Fletcher	Ljungberg
Scholes	Silva
Subbed 78 mins (Carrick)	Fabregas
O'Shea	Hleb
Ronaldo	*Subbed 68 mins (Baptista)*
Rooney	Adebayor
Subbed 77 mins (Solskjaer)	*Subbed 88 mins (Flamini)*
Saha	*sub: Baptista*
sub: Evra	*sub: Flamini*
sub: Carrick	*Subs not used: Almunia, Hoyte, Walcott*
sub: Solskjaer	
Subs not used: Heaton, Vidic	*Coach: Arsene Wenger*
Coach: Sir Alex Ferguson	

READING	MANCHESTER UNITED
Hahnemann	Van der Sar
Murty	Neville
Subbed 89 mins (Bikey)	Vidic
Sonko	Ferdinand
Ingimarsson	Heinze
Shorey	*Subbed 70 mins (O'Shea)*
Ki-Hyeon Seol	Fletcher
Subbed 85 mins (Hunt)	*Subbed 70 mins (Solskjaer)*
Sidwell	Carrick
Harper	Scholes
Convey	Richardson
Lita	*Subbed 58 mins (Saha)*
Subbed 76 mins (Gunnarsson)	Ronaldo
Doyle	Rooney
sub: Bikey	*sub: O'Shea*
sub: Hunt	*sub: Solskjaer*
sub: Gunnarsson	*sub: Saha*
Subs not used: Stack, Long	*Subs not used: Kuszczak, Brown*
Coach: Steve Coppell	*Coach: Sir Alex Ferguson*

6 READING 1
MANCHESTER UNITED 1

FA PREMIERSHIP

DATE: Saturday September 23

ATTENDANCE: 24,098 (Madjeski Stadium)

REFEREE: Peter Walton

GOALS: 48 MINS (1-0) DOYLE - penalty. Awarded after Gary Neville's arm interrupted Graham Murty's cross. Kevin Doyle struck the ball to Van der Sar's right which ended up in the net despite the United goalkeeper getting his fingertips to the ball; **73 MINS (1-1) RONALDO** - equalised with a superb individual goal turning inside right-back Murty and fired superbly past Marcus Hahnemann.

THE GAME: Reading, managed by ex-United player Steve Coppell, tested their illustrious visitors with a positive performance and led the game shortly after half-time. United began the match with a five-man midfield with Rooney as the lone striker. For too long he was left isolated even though United dominated possession and did create 18 attempts on goal, but many were half-chances. United salvaged a point through a brilliant solo goal from Ronaldo – once again booed by the home crowd – who caused so many problems for Reading and their captain Murty in particular! The result meant that Chelsea, who were 2-0 winners at Fulham, now led the Premiership table.

GRAHAM MURTY [ON RONALDO] "Leave him alone, for God's sake - you'll make him angry. He gets a lot of stick from the fans so he's had to become stronger. You've got to try and get close to him but you can't because his feet are that quick and when you do get close he lays it off and goes in behind because he's rapid as well."

SIR ALEX FERGUSON: "We've had a solid start to the season. I was disappointed to drop points last Sunday, but I wasn't disappointed here."

7 MANCHESTER UNITED 2
NEWCASTLE UNITED 0

FA PREMIERSHIP

DATE: Sunday October 1

ATTENDANCE: 75,664 (Old Trafford)

REFEREE: Mike Dean

GOALS: 41 MINS (1-0) SOLSKJAER - side-footed home from six yards after Ronaldo had sprinted across the penalty area. He avoided three challenges before firing a low shot that hit the post and rebounded back to the Norwegian to score; **49 MINS (2-0) SOLSKJAER** - deflected Nemanja Vidic's shot past the goalkeeper.

THE GAME: Manchester United returned to the top of the Premiership on goal difference after a 2-0 victory over a Newcastle side that sought, but clearly failed, to stifle the threat of Ronaldo and Rooney with a packed midfield. Ronaldo was once again unstoppable and he could have had a hat-trick – only to see his three best efforts all hit the woodwork! Newcastle, once again struggling at the wrong end of the table, tried everything to stop Ronaldo, which led to bookings for skipper Scott Parker, and defenders Stephen Carr and Steven Taylor, all for fouls on the Portuguese international. Toon stand-in goalkeeper Steve Harper did his best to keep the home side at bay but goals were inevitable. The goal-hero on the day was Solskjaer with two opportunist goals – one from a rebound and another with a deflection. Down at Stamford Bridge, Chelsea were held to a 1-1 draw by Aston Villa.

GLENN ROEDER: "Everyone is finding it difficult to cope with Ronaldo. It's not an attractive sight if you're a right-back, seeing Ronaldo running at you. He's in scintillating form and, no matter what game United are involved in, he's very much their focal point, along with Rooney. United have two of the finest talents in the world."

MANCHESTER UTD	NEWCASTLE UNITED
Van der Sar	Harper
Neville	Carr
Vidic	Ramage
Ferdinand	Moore
Heinze	Taylor
Subbed 31 mins (Evra)	Milner
Fletcher	*Subbed HT (N'Zogbia)*
Carrick	Butt
Scholes	*Subbed 62 mins (Martins)*
Ronaldo	Emre
Rooney	*Subbed 69 mins (Pattison)*
Solskjaer	Parker
sub: Evra	Duff
Subs not used: Kuszczak, Brown, Saha, O'Shea	Ameobi
Coach: Sir Alex Ferguson	*sub: N'Zogbia*
	sub: Martins
	sub: Pattison
	Subs not used: Krul, Luque
	Coach: Glenn Roeder

8 WIGAN ATHLETIC 1
MANCHESTER UNITED 3

FA PREMIERSHIP

DATE: Saturday October 14

ATTENDANCE: 20,631 (JJB Stadium)

REFEREE: Steve Bennett

GOALS: 5 MINS (1-0) BAINES - beat Van der Sar with 30-yard left-foot shot; **62 MINS (1-1) VIDIC** - headed home, unmarked, from a Giggs corner; **66 MINS (1-2) SAHA** - Gary Teale failed to control the ball and Rooney seized it and sent over a cross that Saha brought down and fired home; **90 MINS (1-3) SOLSKJAER** - netted with precision from Rooney's flick on.

THE GAME: Injury had ruled out Gabriel Heinze, Silvestre, Neville, Park and Ronaldo while Giggs, recovering from a hamstring injury was on the bench. United, showing some caution, began with a five-man midfield with Rooney on the left and Saha as the lone striker. Within five minutes United were trailing to a Wigan side that held their lead beyond half-time. At the break Giggs was introduced and Rooney was paired in attack with Saha. The transformation was stunning with Giggs and Rooney in outstanding form. Rooney, in particular, showed great movement in the final third of the field, creating goals for Saha and Solskjaer, as well as going close including one effort that hit the crossbar as United ran out deserving 3-1 winners.

WAYNE ROONEY: "My form is getting better; I was pleased with how I played against Wigan... I think I'm more or less back to my best and my performances are okay."

PAUL JEWELL [ON ROONEY]: "In my opinion he's the best player in the world. I just can't believe what people have been saying about him. But I don't think he cares less. He won't care what I say, what you say or what the television people say. He's got such strong belief in himself it doesn't matter to him. He couldn't give a toss."

SIR ALEX FERGUSON: "That's Wayne's best performance in a United shirt this season, especially the second half. With Louis Saha he was a real handful."

WIGAN ATHLETIC	MANCHESTER UNITED
Kirkland	Van der Sar
Boyce	Brown
Hall	*Subbed HT (Giggs)*
De Zeeuw	Ferdinand
Baines	Vidic
Teale	Evra
Subbed 69 mins (Valencia)	Solskjaer
Landzaat	Carrick
Scharner	O'Shea
Kilbane	Scholes
Subbed 69 mins (Todorov)	Rooney
Camara	Saha
Subbed 60 mins (McCulloch)	*sub: Giggs*
Heskey	
sub: Valencia	*Subs not used: Kuszczak, Smith, Richardson, D Jones.*
sub: Todorov	*Coach: Sir Alex Ferguson*
sub: McCulloch	
Subs not used: Pollitt, Jackson	
Coach: Paul Jewell	

9 MANCHESTER UNITED 2 / LIVERPOOL 0

FA PREMIERSHIP

Date: Saturday October 22

Attendance: 75,828 (Old Trafford)

Referee: Graham Poll

Goals: 39 mins (1-0) Scholes - Rooney received a glancing header from Scholes and played it to Giggs who squared it across to the edge of the area. Pepe Reina half-blocked Scholes' finish before Scholes forced it home; 66 mins (2-0) Ferdinand - a Giggs left-wing cross was challenged for by Jamie Carragher and Saha. The ball found its way to the far post where Ferdinand brought it under control and cut inside John Arne Riise, before sweeping a left foot shot into the net.

The Game: Manchester United maintained their lead on goal difference at the top of the Premiership after beating Liverpool without any problem in front of another record-breaking Premiership crowd. The Merseysiders' approach appeared to be one of damage limitation after hopes of a goalless draw evaporated once Scholes, making his 500th appearance for United and giving a Man of the Match performance, opened the scoring in the 39th minute. Rooney was playing his 100th game for the Red Devils while Ronaldo was kept on the bench because of illness.

Paul Scholes: "It was quite special but if it's your 500th or your first match for United, it's a big thing. It doesn't make much difference… that was a big day for us. We had to beat Liverpool to stay up with Chelsea."

MANCHESTER UNITED	LIVERPOOL
Van der Sar	Reina
Neville	Finnan
Subbed 78 mins (O'Shea)	Hyypia
Ferdinand	Carragher
Vidic	Riise
Evra	Gerrard
Subbed 90 mins (Brown)	Sissoko
Fletcher	Alonso
Carrick	*Subbed 70 mins (Crouch)*
Scholes	Gonzalez
Giggs	*Subbed 52 mins (Pennant)*
Rooney	Luis Garcia
Saha	Kuyt
sub: O'Shea	*sub: Crouch*
sub: Brown	*sub: Pennant*
Subs not used: Kuszczak, Ronaldo, Solskjaer	**Subs not used:** Dudek, Warnock, Paletta.
Coach: Sir Alex Ferguson	**Coach:** Rafael Benitez

"THE PRESS HAD CALLED IT A GOAL DROUGHT - TEN GAMES INCLUDING ENGLAND AND EUROPEAN MATCHES SINCE I'D NETTED, BUT THE BOSS SAID, 'JUST KEEP IT SIMPLE AND THE GOALS WILL COME'. I WASN'T WORRIED; I KNEW I WAS CONTRIBUTING TO THE TEAM, MAKING LOTS OF ASSISTS, DOING MY WORK. AND WE WERE SCORING FREELY, BUILDING UP OUR GOAL DIFFERENCE AGAINST CHELSEA. WHAT BETTER WAY TO GET MY SCORING GOING AGAIN THAN TO BAG A HAT-TRICK!"

10 BOLTON WANDERERS 0 / MANCHESTER UNITED 4

FA PREMIERSHIP

Date: Saturday October 28

Attendance: 27,224 (Reebok Stadium)

Referee: Rob Styles

Goals: 10 mins (0-1) Rooney - received a superb chipped pass from Carrick before unleashing a powerful shot past goalkeeper Jussi Jaaskelainen; 16 mins (0-2) Rooney - was the first to a loose ball just outside the area and, with great composure, side-footed home; 82 mins (0-3) Ronaldo - found the net after an impressive run and square-pass by Saha; 89 mins (0-4) Rooney - Abdoulaye Meite was at fault with a poor back pass on to which Rooney pounced and scored with a terrific shot.

The Game: Rooney ended a frustrating ten-match spell without a goal by netting the first Premiership hat-trick of the season. Playing the centre-forward role, he was in blistering form and may have netted more than three goals; indeed, United could have easily doubled their goal tally against their North West rivals . In Sir Alex Ferguson's eyes it was the best United performance for three or four years, giving an indication of how hot they were on the day. The display was indeed entertaining, enthralling and unstoppable straight from the kick-off. The half-time break gave Bolton – who were expected to put up a tougher fight on their home patch – some respite and, indeed, they were more competitive in the second-half. That was until the closing ten minutes when further goals from the Roon and Ronaldo Show handed United a comfortable-looking victory.

Wayne Rooney: "The feeling when the first goal went in was brilliant. It was a relief, especially as I had gone such a long time without scoring. To finish the hat-trick was nice."

Louis Saha: "The people who questioned Wayne really don't know anything about football. He has answered everyone with his goals. He's a terrific player, a great. We never doubted him once."

Sir Alex Ferguson: "Once he got the first one, you could see the confidence coming back and after that, I was just hoping the ball would go to him all the time."

BOLTON WANDERERS	MANCHESTER UNITED
Jaaskelainen	Van der Sar
Hunt	Neville
Subbed 69 mins (Pedersen)	Ferdinand
Faye	Vidic
Meite	Evra
Ben Haim	*Subbed 61 mins (Heinze)*
Giannakopoulos	Ronaldo
Subbed 83 mins (Tal)	Carrick
Campo	Scholes
Speed	Giggs
Diouf	*Subbed 83 mins (Fletcher)*
Davies	Saha
Subbed 85 mins (Smith)	*Subbed 82 mins (O'Shea)*
Anelka	Rooney
sub: Pedersen	*sub: Heinze*
sub: Tal	*sub: Fletcher*
sub: Smith	*sub: O'Shea*
Subs not used: Walker, Vaz Te	**Subs not used:** Kuszczak, Solskjaer
Coach: Sam Alladyce	**Coach:** Sir Alex Ferguson

After missing a big chunk of the previous season with an eye injury, Paul Scholes stormed back to score on his 500th appearance for United, against rivals Liverpool

11 | MANCHESTER UNITED 3 PORTSMOUTH 0

FA PREMIERSHIP

DATE: Saturday November 4

ATTENDANCE: 76,004 (Old Trafford)

REFEREE: Mike Dean

GOALS: 3 MINS (1-0) SAHA - penalty. Converted after Stefanovic was adjudged to have brought down Rooney; 10 MINS (2-0) RONALDO - a brilliantly struck free kick of power and precision from 25 yards after Andy O'Brien had fouled Saha; 66 MINS (3-0) VIDIC - header past David James from Neville's right-wing cross.

THE GAME: Manchester United, just four days short of Sir Alex Ferguson's 20th anniversary in charge at Old Trafford, were unchanged in personnel and performance. Within ten minutes they were 2-0 up with Rooney at his direct best winning United's first penalty of the season in the third minute. Fourth-placed Portsmouth had to thank goalkeeper James from preventing United winning by an embarrassing landslide. His saves kept the score down but barely relieved the pressure of the relentless United attack. With Chelsea losing at Tottenham for the first time in 16 years, United established a three-point lead at the top of the table.

SIR ALEX FERGUSON: "We are on the cusp of creating a great team."

MANCHESTER UNITED	PORTSMOUTH
Van der Sar	James
Neville	Pamarot
Ferdinand	O'Brien
Vidic	Stefanovic
Evra	Taylor
Ronaldo	Pedro Mendes
Subbed 75 mins (Fletcher)	Davis
Carrick	Kranjcar
Subbed 71 mins (Silvestre)	*Subbed 84 mins (Hughes)*
Scholes	Fernandes
Giggs	*Subbed HT (Cole)*
Rooney	O'Neil
Subbed 75 mins (O'Shea)	Mwaruwani
Saha	*Subbed 66 mins (LuaLua)*
sub: Fletcher	*sub: Hughes*
sub: Silvestre	*sub: Cole*
sub: O'Shea	*sub: LuaLua*
Subs not used: Kuszczak, Brown	*Subs not used: Kiely, Kanu*
Coach: Sir Alex Ferguson	*Coach: Harry Redknapp*

12 | BLACKBURN ROVERS 0 MANCHESTER UNITED 1

FA PREMIERSHIP

DATE: Saturday November 11

ATTENDANCE: 26,162 (Ewood Park)

REFEREE: Mike Riley

GOAL: 64 MINS (0-1) SAHA - John O'Shea's cross, set up by Rooney, was turned back into the six-yard box by Giggs at the far post. Saha then showed his predatory instincts to hook the ball home.

THE GAME: United's first League win at Rovers' Ewood Park ground since 1998 was more convincing that the single goal margin of victory suggested. Chances were created throughout the game, with Rooney frustrated on three occasions by his own finishing. He also thought he had a legitimate claim for a penalty, but his appeal was turned down by referee Mike Riley. Blackburn's Australian right-back Lucas Neill was given a torrid time by Ronaldo while goalkeeper Brad Friedel was always busy. Rovers' best chance came from Morten Gamst Pedersen, when the lively midfielder saw his in-swinging corner come crashing back off the crossbar.

MARK HUGHES: "It's as good as I've seen United for a good few seasons. The angles of their passing, their rotation of movement, the interchanging, they just pick you off... Ruud van Nistelrooy was a big player for them but him going has released Saha and Rooney. Maybe that partnership has the potential to develop more than Rooney and Van Nistelrooy. Saha has got more pace and is more of a threat attacking-wise. This side, without Van Nistelrooy, is more dynamic."

BLACKBURN ROVERS	MANCHESTER UNITED
Friedel	Van der Sar
Emerton	Neville
Ooijer	*Subbed HT (O'Shea)*
Khizanishvili	Ferdinand
Neill	Vidic
Bentley	Evra
Subbed 79 mins (Peter)	*Subbed 89 mins (Silvestre)*
Mokoena	Ronaldo
Tugay	*Subbed 90 mins (Fletcher)*
Pedersen	Carrick
Nonda	Scholes
Subbed 84 mins (Jeffers)	Giggs
McCarthy	Rooney
sub: Peter	Saha
sub: Jeffers	*sub: O'Shea*
Subs not used: Brown, Henchoz, Gray	*sub: Silvestre*
Coach: Mark Hughes	*sub: Fletcher*
	Subs not used: Kuszczak, Brown
	Coach: Sir Alex Ferguson

"**DURING THE SEASON, A LOT OF PEOPLE WERE REMARKING ON THE BOSS'S GOOD NATURE, SMILING ALL THE TIME, SIGNING LOADS OF AUTOGRAPHS, BEING KIND TO THE PRESS. WELL MOST OF THEM. I SUPPOSE THE BOSS WAS HAPPIER THAN THE PREVIOUS SEASON, AS FAR AS THE OUTSIDE WORLD WAS CONCERNED**"

13 | SHEFFIELD UNITED 1 MANCHESTER UNITED 2

FA PREMIERSHIP

DATE: Saturday November 18

ATTENDANCE: 32,584 (Bramall Lane)

REFEREE: Mark Clattenburg

GOALS: 13 MINS (1-0) GILLESPIE - ex-United player Keith Gillespie headed home a Derek Geary cross; 30 MINS (1-1) ROONEY - latched on to Neville's superb left foot through ball, controlled the pass with one left-foot touch and fired home past Paddy Kenny with the second right foot shot; 75 MINS (1-2) ROONEY - beat goalkeeper with an excellent volley set up by Patrice Evra's left-wing cross that eluded defender Claude Davis.

THE GAME: Two goals from Rooney saw United achieve victory after going behind to a Gillespie goal. Claude Davis was given the task of dealing with Rooney but the Manchester United forward could not be contained and his marker had a hard time of it. Rooney equalised on the half hour but victory was not clinched until he volleyed home with 15 minutes remaining. It was the goal, after much patient play, that blunted the Blades and United could have increased their margin of victory but Ronaldo hit the crossbar. Then, near the end, he missed a sitter while Scholes had one effort cleared off the line. Goalkeeper Paddy Kenny also denied Scholes again with a superb save.

NEIL WARNOCK: "Two great finishes. He is the king. Rooney is the king in our eyes... if you play Rooney there then you're going to score a few goals... when you are our best player in England and one of the best players in the world then it does hurt you when you get criticised. I think he's answered that in the right way. You don't see the nastiness in him. He's more controlled in that respect."

SHEFFIELD UNITED	MANCHESTER UNITED
Kenny	Van der Sar
Kozluk	Neville
Davis	Ferdinand
Jagielka	Vidic
Geary	Evra
Gillespie	*Subbed 80 mins (Heinze)*
Law	Ronaldo
Leigertwood	Carrick
Quinn	Scholes
Subbed 86 mins (Kabba)	Giggs
Kazim-Richards	Rooney
Subbed 79 mins (Nade)	Saha
Hulse	*sub: Heinze*
sub: Kabba	*Subs not used: Kuszczak, O'Shea, Fletcher, Silvestre*
sub: Nade	*Coach: Sir Alex Ferguson*
Subs not used: Morgan, Sommell, Montgomery	
Coach: Neil Warnock	

Captains Phil and Gary Neville lead out their teams. It's the first time brothers have captained opposing sides in the Premiership

MIDDLESBROUGH	MANCHESTER UNITED
Schwarzer	Van der Sar
Huth	Neville
Woodgate	Ferdinand
Subbed HT (Morrison)	Vidic
Pogatetz	Heinze
Xavier	Ronaldo
Subbed 88 mins (Parnaby)	*Subbed 86 mins (Brown)*
Taylor	Scholes
Boateng	Giggs
Cattermole	Fletcher
Downing	*Subbed 75 mins (O'Shea)*
Yakubu	Rooney
Christie	Saha
Subbed 72 mins (Maccarone)	*sub: Brown*
sub: Morrison	*sub: O'Shea*
sub: Parnaby	*Subs not used: Kuszczak,*
sub: Maccarone	*Evra, Carrick*
Subs not used: Jones, Arca	*Coach: Sir Alex Ferguson*
Coach: Gareth Southgate	

14
MANCHESTER UNITED 1
CHELSEA 1

FA PREMIERSHIP

DATE: Saturday November 18

ATTENDANCE: 75,498 (Old Trafford)

REFEREE: Howard Webb

GOALS: 29 MINS (1-0) SAHA - a superb pass by Rooney from inside the centre circle found Saha. Ricardo Carvalho backed off, allowing Saha to unleash a low 20-yard left foot shot that beat Carlo Cudicini at his near post; **69 MINS (1-1)** CARVALHO - out-jumped Heinze to head goalward from Frank Lampard's corner. The ball skimmed Saha's head and went in off the underside of the crossbar.

THE GAME: An engaging and exciting encounter between the Premiership's top two sides saw the spoils perhaps deservedly shared. Both sides had players who shined with Carrick, Vidic, Saha and Rooney particularly notable for United. Indeed it was Rooney who set up Saha to give United a first-half lead while Vidic did a good containment job on Didier Drogba. For Chelsea, Michael Essien was inspirational and Carvalho was the defending champion's saviour at the back.

SIR ALEX FERGUSON: "It was a big opportunity for us but we didn't get the breaks… they didn't make any chances but we should have been a bit more positive. But the most important thing is that we proved we deserved to be in top place in the League."

JOSE MOURINHO: "United lost a big, big chance to open up a six-point lead… if I was in there place I would be very disappointed."

MANCHESTER UNITED	CHELSEA
Van der Sar	Cudicini
Neville	Geremi
Ferdinand	*Subbed HT (Robben)*
Vidic	Carvalho
Heinze	Terry
Ronaldo	A Cole
Subbed 86 mins (Fletcher)	Essien
Carrick	Makelele
Scholes	Ballack
Giggs	*Subbed 90 mins (Ferreira)*
Rooney	Lampard
Saha	Shevchenko
Subbed 86 mins (O'Shea)	*Subbed 75 mins (J Cole)*
sub: Fletcher	Drogba
sub: O'Shea	*sub: Robben*
Subs not used: Kuszczak,	*sub: Ferreira*
Evra, Silvestre	*sub: J Cole*
Coach: Sir Alex Ferguson	*Subs not used: Hilario,*
	Boulahrouz
	Coach: Jose Mourinho

16
MIDDLESBROUGH 1
MANCHESTER UNITED 2

FA PREMIERSHIP

DATE: Saturday December 2

ATTENDANCE: 31,238 (Riverside Stadium)

REFEREE: Chris Foy

GOALS: 19 MINS (0-1) SAHA - penalty. Referee Foy adjudged that goalkeeper Mark Schwarzer had brought down Ronaldo and Saha converted the spot kick; **66 MINS (1-1)** MORRISON - Stewart Downing created the chance with a left-wing cross which deflected off Heinze to James Morrison, who shot home from ten yards; **68 MINS (1-2)** FLETCHER - Scholes intercepted Downing's pass and then played it to Ronaldo. He in turn gave to Giggs, who crossed for Fletcher to net with a close range header.

THE GAME: Manchester United, inspired by midfielder Scholes, deservedly claimed their seventh away win in eight games, although not without controversy. The deadlock was broken when Ronaldo won a penalty after appearing to be fouled by Aussie goalkeeper Schwarzer (TV replays showed it was a harsh decision on the home side). Saha converted the penalty but an aggrieved Middlesbrough briefly fought back, hitting the woodwork through defender Abel Xavier shortly afterwards. Level terms were briefly attained in the second-half until Fletcher restored the lead. United had created plenty of chances, with Saha denied on the line by defender Robert Huth, while Giggs missed a sitter in front of an empty net.

GARY NEVILLE: "I just have a feeling now we are not going to fall away."

SIR ALEX FERGUSON: "It was a penalty."

GARETH SOUTHGATE: "It was always a very tough game for us, they're the best side at the moment in the League, but obviously it's made a lot harder when you go behind to a goal like that… it's very difficult for the referee because it happens very quickly but how many times are we going to see it? The lad has got a history of doing it. I think in the end it cost us the game. Our goalkeeper has done everything he can to get out the way, there's clearly no contact - I didn't think so at the time and obviously when you see the replays there's nothing there - and the lad goes down once again. For me it's never a penalty."

15
MANCHESTER UNITED 3
EVERTON 0

FA PREMIERSHIP

DATE: Sunday November 29

ATTENDANCE: 75,723 (Old Trafford)

REFEREE: Mark Halsey

GOALS: 39 MINS (1-0) RONALDO - fired a low shot past goalkeeper Richard Wright after a Carrick shot had rebounded off Nuno Valente; **63 MINS (2-0)** EVRA - Rooney slotted ball through defence for Evra, darting behind Joseph Yobo and beating the offside trap, before firing his shot underneath Wright; **89 MINS (3-0)** O'SHEA - clipped the ball past goalkeeper Wright from Evra's left-wing cross.

THE GAME: The match had the distinction of two sides being captained by two brothers - Gary and Phil Neville. Sir Alex Ferguson made five changes to the side that drew with Chelsea demoting Heinze, Saha and Scholes to the bench while Giggs and Vidic were rested. United, however, did not play well but still ran out comfortable winners simply because Everton were not a threat. Rooney, for his part, had opportunities to score but was denied by his own poor finishing or the goalkeeping of Wright. Ronaldo opened the scoring while Patrice Evra scored his first goal for United and then set up the third for O'Shea.

SIR ALEX FERGUSON: "We had to make changes and we've got away with it."

MANCHESTER UNITED	EVERTON
Van der Sar	Wright
G Neville	Yobo
Ferdinand	Stubbs
Silvestre	Lescott
Evra	Nuno Valente
Fletcher	Arteta
Carrick	P Neville
Subbed 73 mins (Brown)	Carsley
O'Shea	Osman
Richardson	*(76 mins Vaughan)*
Rooney	Beattie
Ronaldo	McFadden
Subbed 68 mins (Heinze)	*sub: Vaughan*
sub: Brown	*Subs not used: Ruddy, Weir,*
sub: Heinze	*Van der Meyde, Anichebe*
Subs not used: Kuszczak,	*Coach: David Moyes*
Saha, Scholes	
Coach: Sir Alex Ferguson	

17 | MANCHESTER UNITED 3 / MANCHESTER CITY 1

FA PREMIERSHIP

DATE: Saturday December 9

ATTENDANCE: 75,858 (Old Trafford)

REFEREE: Graham Poll

GOALS: 6 MINS (1-0) ROONEY - City's Sylvain Distin failed to cut out Ronaldo's low cross and allowed Rooney to shoot home; **45 MINS (2-0) SAHA** - Heinze's cross eluded the City defence and allowed Saha to turn the ball past goalkeeper Nicky Weaver; **72 MINS (2-1) TRABELSI** - Stephen Ireland turned Vidic and set up Hatem Trabelsi to score with swerving left foot shot; **84 MINS (3-1) RONALDO** - another cross, this time from Rooney, was not intercepted by Richard Dunne and Ronaldo was free to beat the goalkeeper.

THE GAME: With the exception of a 12-minute second-half spell when City halved United's lead, the outcome was never in doubt in the 135th Mancunian derby. Rooney gave United a sixth minute lead and it was surprising it took until the stroke of half-time for United to increase the margin. Rooney and Ronaldo taunted the City defence throughout and were kept at bay by magnificent goalkeeping displays by Weaver and, in particular, substitute 'keeper Andreas Isaksson. City were a minimum threat and it got worse for the visitors with the sending-off by Bernado Corradi in the last minute for a second bookable offence, namely, diving in the penalty box. The win moved United nine points clear at the top of the Premiership table.

SIR ALEX FERGUSON: "We're playing well and I think they know that. We can relax and watch Sunday's game at Chelsea and support the Gunners for a change!"

MANCHESTER UNITED	MANCHESTER CITY
Van der Sar	Weaver
Neville	*Subbed HT (Isaksson)*
Ferdinand	Richards
Vidic	*Subbed 76 mins (Beasley)*
Heinze	Dunne
Ronaldo ⚽	Distin
Carrick	Thatcher
Scholes	Trabelsi ⚽
Giggs	Reyna
Rooney ⚽	*Subbed HT (Ireland)*
Saha ⚽	Barton
Subbed 66 mins (O'Shea)	Vassell
sub: *O'Shea*	Corradi
	Samaras
Subs not used: *Kuszczak, Solskjaer, Fletcher, Silvestre*	**Subs not used:** *Dickov, Onouha*
Coach: *Sir Alex Ferguson*	**Coach:** *Stuart Pearce*

Gabriel Agbonlahor and Nemanja Vidic battle it out during United's win at Villa Park

19 | ASTON VILLA 0 / MANCHESTER UNITED 3

FA PREMIERSHIP

DATE: Saturday December 23

ATTENDANCE: 42,551 (Villa Park)

REFEREE: Steve Bennett

GOALS: 58 MINS (0-1) RONALDO - ran from inside his own half and then hit a shot that was deflected off Gary Cahill. The rebound ran back to Ronaldo and he hit a venomous drive inside Gabor Kiraly's near post; **64 MINS (0-2) SCHOLES** - hit a truly stunning volley in off the underside of the crossbar from Gavin McCann's headed clearance; **85 MINS (0-3) RONALDO** - finished off a move created by Giggs and involving Scholes, Rooney and Neville, with a tap in at the far post.

THE GAME: Manchester United needed patience to overcome a battling Aston Villa side. After an indifferent first-half United sparkled after the break and the opening goal – the 2,000th United goal under Sir Alex Ferguson – appeared to send Villa into disarray. Two-goal hero Ronaldo was as illuminating as ever giving all sorts of problems to defender Aaron Hughes. Rooney was on the bench but came on in the 66th minute and was involved in the build-up to United's third goal.

MARTIN O'NEILL: "We were playing very well until they scored, which was avoidable from our point of view. Make a mistake against a quality side and you'll remember it."

ASTON VILLA	MANCHESTER UNITED
Kiraly	Van der Sar
Hughes	Neville
Mellberg	Vidic
Cahill	Ferdinand
Barry	Evra
Agbonlahor	Ronaldo ⚽⚽
McCann	Fletcher
Subbed 76 mins (Angel)	Park
Gardner	*Subbed 66 mins (Rooney)*
Petrov	Scholes ⚽
Davis	*Subbed 88 mins (Silvestre)*
Sutton	Giggs
sub: Angel	*Subbed 88 mins (O'Shea)*
Subs not used: *Olejnik, Baros, Bouma, Ridgewell*	Saha
Coach: *Martin O'Neill*	**Subs not used:** *Kuszczak, Brown.*
	sub: Rooney
	sub: Silvestre
	sub: O'Shea
	Subs not used: *Kuczszak, Silvestre*
	Coach: *Sir Alex Ferguson*

18 | WEST HAM UNITED 1 / MANCHESTER UNITED 0

FA PREMIERSHIP

DATE: Sunday December 17

ATTENDANCE: 34,966 (Upton Park)

REFEREE: Phil Dowd

GOALS: 75 MINS (1-0) REO-COKER - former United hero Teddy Sheringham slipped a pass through Vidic's legs towards the near post. Marlon Harewood picked the ball up, turned Ferdinand then cut back for Nigel Reo-Coker to shoot into the net.

THE GAME: West Ham, with Alan Curbishley in charge for the first time, ended a disconcerting week for United by inflicting their second Premiership defeat of the season. With Chelsea having won in midweek and claiming a late victory at Everton earlier in the day the United lead was a slender two points. United did create several chances but Hammers goalkeeper Robert Green was in superb form and skipper Reo-Coker impressed with a match-winning goal.

SIR ALEX FERGUSON: "We didn't deserve to lose but we have to gather ourselves and start another charge. We have to show our mettle. That's the true mark of champions and we've proved it in the past."

WEST HAM UNITED	MANCHESTER UNITED
Green	Van der Sar
Spector	Neville
A Ferdinand	R Ferdinand
Collins	Vidic
Konchesky	Heinze
Bowyer	*(88 mins Park)*
Reo-Coker ⚽	Ronaldo
Mullins	Carrick
Subbed 71 mins (Benayoun)	*Subbed 84 mins (O'Shea)*
Etherington	Scholes
Subbed 77 mins (McCartney)	Giggs
Harewood	*Subbed 73 mins (Solskjaer)*
Zamora	Rooney
Subbed 59 mins (Sheringham)	Saha
sub: Benayoun	*sub: Park*
sub: McCartney	*sub: O'Shea*
sub: Sheringham	*sub: Solskjaer*
Subs not used: *Carroll, Tevez*	**Subs not used:** *Kuczszak, Silvestre*
Coach: *Alan Curbishley*	**Coach:** *Sir Alex Ferguson*

"I WAS PUT ON THE BENCH FOR ONE GAME, AGAINST ASTON VILLA. I HADN'T BEEN PLAYING AS WELL AS I COULD AND THE BOSS SAID HE WAS JUST GIVING ME A REST, THAT WAS ALL. HE WOULD BE DOING IT WITH OTHER PLAYERS AS THE SEASON PROGRESSED. I WAS DISAPPOINTED. I ALWAYS WANT TO PLAY, REGARDLESS, BUT I DIDN'T DWELL ON IT OR SEE IT AS A BAD SIGN"

20
MANCHESTER UNITED 3
WIGAN ATHLETIC 1

FA PREMIERSHIP

DATE: Tuesday December 26

ATTENDANCE: 76,018 (Old Trafford)

REFEREE: Mike Riley

GOALS: 47 MINS (1-0) RONALDO - headed home a Scholes corner; 51 MINS (2-0) RONALDO - Park dispossessed defender Teale inside Wigan's penalty area and then was fouled. Ronaldo took the penalty which goalkeeper Chris Kirkland saved but could do nothing with the follow-up from the rebound; 59 MINS (3-0) SOLSKJAER - Rooney's header sent Solskjaer racing forward, escaping defender Fitz Hall before slipping the ball past Kirkland; 90 MINS (3-1) BAINES - penalty. Full-back Leighton converted after Silvestre had fouled David Wright in stoppage time.

THE GAME: Just as the two sides emerged from the tunnel the news came through that Chelsea had been held to a 2-2 draw by Reading. United rested Ferdinand and Giggs while Ronaldo began on the bench. United were outstanding from the kick-off, creating a whole host of chances with Rooney having the lion's share of the opportunities. Wigan goalkeeper Kirkland was in good form in keeping Rooney and Co at bay throughout the first-half. Ronaldo was introduced after the break and within 69 seconds he had broke the deadlock; by the 49th minute he had a penalty saved by Kirkland; two minutes later Ronaldo had made it 2-0. Just before the hour mark it was 3-0. Rooney almost made it four but hit the crossbar. A comfortable victory – despite Baines' last-minute penalty conversion – that extended United's Premiership lead to four points.

SIR ALEX FERGUSON: "Jose said last week we will drop points but he doesn't seem to realise that they will drop points also. That's the nature of football; it can knock you on your head. We certainly didn't expect them to draw... the key is consistency and, if we can maintain the consistency we have shown in the first half of the season, we have a marvellous chance."

MANCHESTER UNITED	WIGAN ATHLETIC
Van der Sar	Kirkland
Brown	Boyce
Vidic	Jackson
Silvestre	Hall
Evra	Subbed 60 mins (Skoko)
Subbed 70 mins (Heinze)	Baines
Fletcher	Teale
Subbed HT (Ronaldo)	Subbed 52 mins (Cotterill)
O'Shea	Johansson
Scholes	Wright
Subbed 62 mins (Richardson)	Kilbane
Park	Todorov
Rooney	Heskey
Solskjaer	sub: Skoko
sub: Heinze	sub: Cotterill
sub: Ronaldo	Subs not used: Pollitt, Landzaat, Cywka
sub: Richardson	Coach: Paul Jewell
Subs not used: Kuszczak, Saha	
Coach: Sir Alex Ferguson	

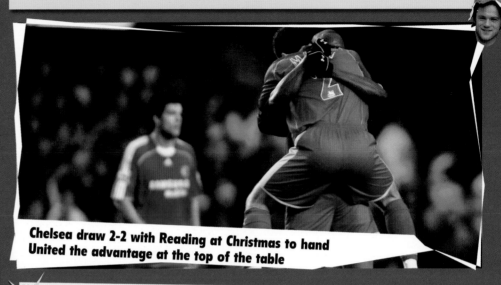

Chelsea draw 2-2 with Reading at Christmas to hand United the advantage at the top of the table

21
MANCHESTER UNITED 3
READING 2

FA PREMIERSHIP

DATE: Saturday December 30

ATTENDANCE: 75,910 (Old Trafford)

REFEREE: Mike Dean

GOALS: 33 MINS (1-0) SOLSKJAER - Ronaldo duped Glen Little before hitting over a cross for Solskjaer, who evaded Ibrahima Sonko, to open the scoring with a header from six yards; 38 MINS (1-1) SONKO - a Nicky Shorey free kick saw Van der Sar come out for and miss, allowing Sonko to head home; 59 MINS (2-1) RONALDO - Giggs and Rooney combined to set up Solskjaer, who shot against the post, Ronaldo pounced on the rebound and netted; 77 MINS (3-1) RONALDO - Giggs pinpoint cross for Ronaldo to side-foot home at the far post; 90 MINS (3-2) LITA - striker Leroy easily knocked Silvestre off the ball on his way to scoring.

THE GAME: A thoroughly exciting match which saw 10-man Reading stage a magnificent fight-back that just fell short of sharing the points. United, without the suspended Scholes and Vidic, were in brilliant form with Ronaldo once again shining brightly and Solskjaer also impressing in a fantastic team performance. Plenty of goalscoring opportunities were created and United's goal tally could have been greater than three. The dismissal of substitute Sam Sodje for two bookable offences quickly followed by United's third goal confirmed United's superiority. Then amazingly under-manned Reading staged a tenacious fight-back to 3-2 but ran out of time to complete the task and salvage point.

The win, on the eve of Sir Alex Ferguson's 65th birthday, coupled with Chelsea being held at home by Fulham, saw United extend their Premiership lead to eight points.

SIR ALEX FERGUSON: "That was our worst defending of the season. We went to sleep at the end, but of course I'm delighted to be six points clear. I've always said that if we could go into the New Year on top we would have an outstanding chance."

MANCHESTER UNITED	READING
Van der Sar	Hahnemann
Brown	Murty
Ferdinand	Subbed 59 mins (Sodje)
Silvestre	Sonko
Heinze	Ingimarsson
Ronaldo	Shorey
Subbed 78 mins (Fletcher)	Little
O'Shea	Subbed 66 mins (Seol)
Carrick	Sidwell
Park	Gunnarsson
Subbed HT (Giggs)	Harper
Rooney	Doyle
Subbed 79 mins (Richardson)	Subbed 73 mins (Hunt)
Solskjaer	Lita
sub: Fletcher	sub: Sodje
sub: Giggs	sub: Seol
sub: Richardson	sub: Hunt
Subs not used: Kuszczak, Saha	Subs not used: Federici, Oster
Coach: Sir Alex Ferguson	Coach: Steve Coppell

22
NEWCASTLE UNITED 2
MANCHESTER UNITED 2

FA PREMIERSHIP

DATE: Monday January 1, 2007

ATTENDANCE: 52,302 (St James' Park)

REFEREE: Rob Styles

GOALS: 33 MINS (1-0) MILNER - Midfielder James cut inside Neville and created enough space to hit a rising shot from 20 yards that beat Van der Sar; 40 MINS (1-1) SCHOLES - a move started by Scholes then moved on by Giggs and Fletcher before being finished off by Scholes with a shot past Shay Given; 46 MINS (1-2) SCHOLES - within 23 seconds of the re-start Scholes fired a low shot that came off Taylor and into the net; 74 MINS (2-2) EDGAR - Newcastle left-back David cut inside and fired a diagonal right-foot shot from 30 yards out that deflected off Scholes, beyond Van der Sar and into the far corner of the net.

THE GAME: Injury-hit Newcastle were tenacious as they battled hard against the Premiership leaders in this see-saw of a fixture. Milner put Newcastle ahead but two goals from Scholes either side of half-time saw Manchester United gain the initiative. Teenager David Edgar scored a spectacular equaliser to earn the Magpies a share of the points. The truth was that for all of Newcastle's endeavour, Manchester United could have sealed victory with Giggs, Saha and Park all having efforts cleared off the line. Park also hit the woodwork while Saha and Rooney were denied by two fines saves from Given. Fortunately, Chelsea did not exploit United's failure to win at St James' Park as the following night the Londoners were held to a goalless draw at Villa Park.

SIR ALEX FERGUSON: "It's a real challenge for the championship. Chelsea are not getting their own way, the way they have done for the last two years... we didn't play as well as we have been but that's because Newcastle didn't allow us to do that, they wanted to be first to every ball."

NEWCASTLE UNITED	MANCHESTER UNITED
Given	Van der Sar
Solano	Neville
Huntington	Vidic
Taylor	Ferdinand
Edgar	Evra
Dyer	Ronaldo
Parker	Fletcher
Emre	Subbed 77 mins (Carrick)
Subbed 87 mins (Pattison)	Scholes
Milner	Giggs
Martins	Rooney
Sibierski	Saha
sub: Pattison	Subbed 36 mins (Park)
Subs not used: Srnicek, Luque, O'Brien, Carroll	sub: Carrick
Coach: Glenn Roeder	Subs not used: Heaton, Heinze, O'Shea
	Coach: Sir Alex Ferguson

23 MANCHESTER UNITED 3 / ASTON VILLA 1

FA PREMIERSHIP

DATE: Saturday January 13

ATTENDANCE: 76,073 (Old Trafford)

REFEREE: Howard Webb

GOALS: 11 MINS (1-0) PARK - Both Aaron Hughes and Gary Cahill failed to clear Neville's right-wing cross, which allowed Park to shoot home at the second attempt; **13 MINS (2-0) CARRICK** - won the ball on the edge of his own area and twice played a one-two with Scholes and then exchanged with Park before volleying the ball into the back of the net; **25 MINS (3-0) RONALDO** - McCann lost possession to Park on the edge of his own area and the subsequent United attack ended with Ronaldo netting a Carrick cross; **52 MINS (3-1) AGBONLAHOR** - Milan Baros, beating Vidic and Evra, provided the assist for Gabby Agbonlahor to score with a simple tap-in.

THE GAME: Manchester United had this match sewn up by the 25th minute with goals from Park, Carrick and Ronaldo. Inevitably there could have been more for the hosts, but for the goalkeeping of Dane Thomas Sorensen. Furthermore, Rooney saw one of his efforts – a curling shot – hit the crossbar while Saha had another effort cleared off the line. Rooney worked as hard as ever while Ronaldo, who picked up his second Premiership Player of the Month Award of the season before the game, was as creative as ever. For Villa it was their 12th game without a win.

SIR ALEX FERGUSON: "He [Rooney] just needs a goal to give him confidence but he is working hard. I have no concerns about him."

MANCHESTER UNITED	ASTON VILLA
Van der Sar	Sorensen
Neville	Mellberg
Vidic	Ridgewell
Ferdinand	Cahill
Evra	Bouma
Ronaldo ⚽	Subbed HT (Samuel)
Carrick ⚽	Hughes
Subbed 80 mins (O'Shea)	Subbed HT (Davis)
Scholes	McCann
Park ⚽	Osbourne
Subbed 65 mins (Saha)	Barry
Larsson	Agbonlahor ⚽
Subbed 80 mins (Solskjaer)	Baros
Rooney	sub: Samuel
sub: O'Shea	sub: Davis
sub: Saha	Subs not used: Taylor, Hendrie, Angel
sub: Solskjaer	Coach: Martin O'Neill
Subs not used: Kuszczak, Giggs	
Coach: Sir Alex Ferguson	

24 ARSENAL 2 / MANCHESTER UNITED 1

FA PREMIERSHIP

DATE: Sunday January 21

ATTENDANCE: 60,128 (Emirates Stadium)

REFEREE: Steve Bennett

GOALS: 53 MINS (0-1) ROONEY - on the left, Ronaldo fed the overlapping Evra, who crossed deep for the unmarked and onrushing Rooney to head home at the far post; **83 MINS (1-1) VAN PERSIE** - a deep right-wing cross from Rosicky found van Persie beyond the far post, from where he found the net with an angled shot; **90 MINS (2-1) HENRY** - Emmanuel Eboue and Rosicky exchanged passes before the former centred for ThierryHenry to head home.

THE GAME: Arsenal came from behind and grabbed a dramatic stoppage winner to complete a Premiership double over United for the season. Rooney had given the visitors the lead after 53 minutes with his first goal in eight matches. He looked to have set them up for another victory and extend their lead at the top of the table following Chelsea's 2-0 defeat at Liverpool the day before. However, the Gunners, who had been off the pace for much of the game, had a sting in their tail and Henry made no mistake with his last-gasp bullet header from Eboue's pin-point cross. The real winners on the day were, of course, a relieved Chelsea.

SIR ALEX FERGUSON: "Teams at the top always drop points on the run in. It happens – but how you cope is important. Only true champions come out and show their worth and I expect us to do that."

ARSENAL	MANCHESTER UNITED
Lehmann	Van der Sar
Eboue	Neville
Subbed 90 mins (Hoyte)	Vidic
Toure	Ferdinand
Senderos	Evra
Clichy	Ronaldo
Hleb	Subbed 90 mins (Heinze)
Subbed 67 mins (van Persie)	Scholes
Fabregas	Carrick
Flamini	Giggs
Subbed 79 mins (Baptista)	Rooney ⚽
Rosicky	Larsson
Adebayor	Subbed 81 mins (Saha)
Henry ⚽	sub: Heinze
sub: Hoyte	sub: Saha
sub: van Persie ⚽	Subs not used: Kuszczak, Brown, Fletcher
sub: Baptista	Coach: Sir Alex Ferguson
Subs not used: Almunia, Denilson	
Coach: Arsene Wenger	

25 MANCHESTER UNITED 4 / WATFORD 0

FA PREMIERSHIP

DATE: Wednesday January 31

ATTENDANCE: 76,032 (Old Trafford)

REFEREE: Mike Dean

GOALS: 20 MINS (1-0) RONALDO - penalty. Ronaldo converted the spot kick after Jay DeMerit had fouled Solskjaer; **61 MINS (2-0) DOYLEY OWN GOAL** - defender Lloyd headed past his own goalkeeper while attempting to cut out Kieron Richardson's cross; **70 MINS (3-0) LARSSON** - played a one-two with Rooney down the middle before firing a shot past Lee into the net; **71 MINS (4-0) ROONEY** - Ronaldo performed an up-and-under over the Watford defence for Rooney to run on to and then lob the ball over the goalkeeper and into the net.

THE GAME: Top versus bottom and the inevitable outcome. Struggling Watford set out to defend in numbers and, to a degree, it worked in the first-half with United only finding the net via the penalty spot. After the break, however, United were unstoppable, netting three goals in a ten-minute spell. Rooney emphasised his return to form by setting up United's third goal for on-loan Larsson, before netting the fourth and final goal himself a minute later. Once again the winning margin could have been much greater but other goalscoring chances were squandered.

MANCHESTER UNITED	WATFORD
Kuszczak	Lee
Neville	Mariappa
Ferdinand	DeMerit
Vidic	Doyley OG
Subbed 75 mins (Silvestre)	Stewart
Heinze	Bangura
Ronaldo ⚽	Francis
Carrick	Bouazza
(75 mins (Brown))	Powell
O'Shea	Subbed 72 mins (Hoskins)
Richardson	Smith
Rooney ⚽	Subbed 72 mins (Williamson)
Solskjaer	Henderson
(64 mins (Larsson))	Subbed 76 mins (Kabba)
sub: Silvestre	sub: Hoskins
sub: Brown	sub: Williamson
sub: Larsson ⚽	sub: Kabba
Subs not used: Van der Sar, Park	Subs not used: Chamberlain, McNamee, Hoskins
Coach: Sir Alex Ferguson	Coach: Adrian Boothroyd

SIR ALEX FERGUSON: "We created and missed a lot of opportunities but I have to be satisfied whenever we win by four goals. Watford set their stall out to defend but it was comfortable for us in the end."

Henrik Larsson, Sir Alex's inspired mid-season signing, scraps with Arsenal's Cesc Fabregas at the Emirates

"IN THE JANUARY TRANSFER WINDOW, HENRIK LARSSON ARRIVED FROM SWEDEN. IN TRAINING HE WAS BRILLIANT, A MODEL PROFESSIONAL. ON THE PITCH HIS MOVEMENT WAS FIRST CLASS. I LEARNED A LOT JUST WATCHING HIM. HIS RUNS WERE ALWAYS SO INTELLIGENT. HE NEVER TAKES MORE THAN TWO TOUCHES AND NEVER GIVES THE BALL AWAY.

"HAITCH — THAT'S WHAT I CALL HENRIK, BY THE WAY — WAS VITAL DURING THE TWO-AND-HALF MONTH SPELL WITH US, ESPECIALLY IN THE EUROPEAN GAMES WITH ALL HIS EXPERIENCE. HE GAVE US ANOTHER OPTION AND SCORED SOME IMPORTANT GOALS"

26 TOTTENHAM HOTSPUR 0
MANCHESTER UNITED 4

FA PREMIERSHIP

DATE: Sunday February 4

ATTENDANCE: 36,164 (White Hart Lane)

REFEREE: Mark Clattenburg

GOALS: 45 MINS (0-1) RONALDO - penalty. Ronaldo fired home a low spot kick past Paul Robinson after Steed Malbranque was adjudged to have brought down the United player; 48 MINS (0-2) VIDIC - Carrick's corner saw Vidic steal in front of Michael Dawson to score with a header; 54 MINS (0-3) SCHOLES - Ronaldo pulled the ball back to the byline but Robinson only palmed his interception, which allowed Scholes to score from close range; 77 MINS (0-4) GIGGS - Saha sent Giggs clear and the Welsh international shot past the England goalkeeper.

THE GAME: Another stunning second-half performance, inspired by Ronaldo, saw Manchester United sweep aside the threat of North Londoners Tottenham. Ronaldo, playing to the inevitable 'theme music' of opposing fans' jeers, had given United the platform they needed for victory by earning and converting a penalty on the stroke of half-time. Vidic, the scorer of United's second goal, was impressive in the heart of the United defence. On the downside for United was the enforced substitution of Rooney with a back injury in the 66th minute and Van der Sar's premature departure after he suffered a broken nose following a collision with Spurs striker Robbie Keane. United had already utilised their three substitutes so goalkeeper and still kept a clean sheet for the visitors.

AARON LENNON (TOTTENHAM): "I would have to say Ronaldo is the player I admire most. He is the best player in the world. The way he plays week in, week out is unbelievable. He's improved so much in the last couple of years. I do look at how he has changed his game."

SIR ALEX FERGUSON: "Zeros against your name is the name of the game because going towards a title race, that's going to be important."

TOTTENHAM HOTSPUR	MANCHESTER UNITED
Robinson	Van der Sar
Chimbonda	Neville
Lee	Vidic ⚽
Dawson	Ferdinand
Gardner	Evra
Huddlestone	Ronaldo ⚽
Lennon	*Subbed 68 mins (Park)*
Zokora	Carrick
Subbed 56 mins (Ghaly)	Scholes ⚽
Malbranque	Giggs ⚽
Defoe	*Subbed 80 mins (O'Shea)*
Subbed 56 mins (Keane)	Rooney
Berbatov	*Subbed 66 mins (Saha)*
sub: Ghaly	Larsson
sub: Keane	*sub: Park*
Subs not used: *Cerny, Murphy, Rocha*	*sub: O'Shea*
	sub: Saha
Coach: *Martin Jol*	**Subs not used:** *Kuszczak, Heinze*
	Coach: *Sir Alex Ferguson*

27 MANCHESTER UNITED 2
CHARLTON 0

FA PREMIERSHIP

DATE: Saturday February 10

ATTENDANCE: 75,883 (Old Trafford)

REFEREE: Mike Riley

GOALS: 24 MINS (1-0) PARK - headed home Evra's deflected left-wing cross; 82 MINS (2-0) FLETCHER - Rooney had a shot blocked by goalkeeper Carson and his second attempt screwed into the path of Fletcher who scored with a diving header.

THE GAME: By recent performances Manchester United appeared a little subdued but still managed to labour to a necessary victory. United were without Van der Sar, Carrick and Ronaldo (who had a cold) while Charlton, to their credit, did not set out simply to defend and attempted, although without much success, to penetrate the United defence. Their best effort from Darren Ambrose forced Kuszczak into a full-length diving save. Park and Fletcher got the goals that mattered for the points but the impressive Rooney almost netted a brilliant goal. The England forward brought Giggs' high ball under control in a move that neutralised three Charlton defenders before unleashing a powerful right-foot shot that goalkeeper Carson had no chance in stopping. Agonisingly for Rooney, his superbly executed effort skimmed the outside of the post.

GARY NEVILLE: "For the last few years we've heard opposition players saying it's a lot easier to come to Old Trafford than it had been in the past. They thought they could come here and get a result and that was sickening for us. We knew we had to get back to making Old Trafford a hard place to visit and I think we have done that this season."

SIR ALEX FERGUSON: "We don't need to look over our shoulders at Chelsea. I don't think we need to do that in our position."

MANCHESTER UNITED	CHARLTON ATHLETIC
Kuszczak	Carson
Neville	Sankofa
Vidic	Diawara
Ferdinand	Bougherra
Evra	Thatcher
Fletcher ⚽	Rommedahl
Scholes	Song
Giggs	Holland
Subbed 62 mins (Larsson)	*Subbed 73 mins (Hughes)*
Park ⚽	Faye
Rooney	*Subbed 40 mins (Zheng)*
Saha	Ambrose
Subbed 81 mins (Richardson)	*Subbed 73 mins (Lisbie)*
sub: Larsson	M Bent
sub: Richardson	*sub: Hughes*
Subs not used: *Heaton, Brown, Silvestre*	*sub: Zheng*
	sub: Lisbie
Coach: *Sir Alex Ferguson*	**Subs not used:** *Randolph, Hasselbaink*
	Coach: *Alan Pardew*

28 FULHAM 1
MANCHESTER UNITED 2

FA PREMIERSHIP

DATE: Saturday February 24

ATTENDANCE: 26,412 (Craven Cottage)

REFEREE: Peter Walton

GOALS: 17 MINS (1-0) McBRIDE - A mix-up between Van der Sar and Vidic allowed Brian McBride to steal in and score from a narrow angle; 29 MINS (1-1) GIGGS - released Rooney down the left. He carried on his forward run on the right to meet Rooney's dipping centre with a cross-shot, from the outside of his left foot, that beat goalkeeper Jan Lastuvka; 88 MINS (1-2) RONALDO - out-paced Moritz Volz and Clint Dempsey on the left before cutting and unleashing a powerful left foot shot from 25 yards that deflected off Philippe Christanval's ankle into the right hand corner of the net.

THE GAME: Fulham severely tested Manchester United and were only denied a draw by Ronaldo's late winner. The Londoners not only took the lead but kept Edwin van der Sar on his toes. He needed to produce some good saves including one superb reaction to deny Simon Davies at the start of the second-half. For United, Giggs, captain in the absence of Neville, provided the drive and leadership necessary to keep United on course – particularly as Scholes had been expertly shackled by Wes Brown. With a draw looking the probable result, Ronaldo found his way through with a terrific match-winning shot.

SIR ALEX FERGUSON: "I have to admit I could not see it coming. Sometimes there are games where you get the feeling you would like to come back another day. I felt like that after two minutes. Our running was poor and the speed of our game was poor. Yet we scored so late on it could be significant. We are in a fantastic position but we have some difficult games left... I am not saying we are going to win but I know for certain we will not play as badly."

FULHAM	MANCHESTER UNITED
Lastuvka	Van der Sar
Volz	Brown
Christanval	Ferdinand
Bocanegra	Vidic
Rosenior	*Subbed 59 mins (O'Shea)*
Davies	Evra
Brown	*(67 mins Silvestre)*
Smertin	Ronaldo ⚽
Diop	Carrick
Subbed 71 mins (Dempsey)	*Subbed 66 mins (Saha)*
McBride ⚽	Scholes
Subbed 79 mins (Helguson)	Giggs ⚽
Radzinski	Larsson
Subbed 72 mins (John)	Rooney
sub: Dempsey	*sub: Dempsey*
sub: Helguson	*sub: Helguson*
sub: John	*sub: John*
Subs not used: *Warner, Routledge*	**Subs not used:** *Kuszczak, Park*
Coach: *Chris Coleman*	**Coach:** *Sir Alex Ferguson*

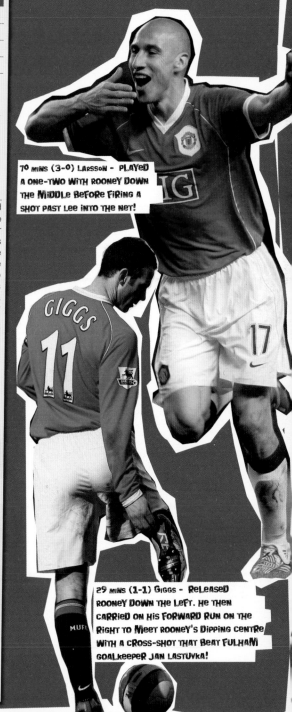

70 MINS (3-0) LARSSON - PLAYED A ONE-TWO WITH ROONEY DOWN THE MIDDLE BEFORE FIRING A SHOT PAST LEE INTO THE NET!

29 MINS (1-1) GIGGS - RELEASED ROONEY DOWN THE LEFT. HE THEN CARRIED ON HIS FORWARD RUN ON THE RIGHT TO MEET ROONEY'S DIPPING CENTRE WITH A CROSS-SHOT THAT BEAT FULHAM GOALKEEPER JAN LASTUVKA!

MANCHESTER UNITED'S MAGICAL SEASON

> "I WAS SITTING IN THE DRESSING ROOM AT ANFIELD WONDERING WHAT WAS GOING ON OUT THERE ON THE PITCH. THE NOISE WAS ABSOLUTELY DEAFENING, ECHOING AROUND THE DRESSING ROOM. I COULD WORK OUT WHEN THE LIVERPOOL FANS WERE PLEASED OR NOT BY THE NOISE, BUT I DIDN'T KNOW WHAT WAS HAPPENING. THERE WAS NO MONITOR IN THE DRESSING ROOM. IT WAS JUST ME, THE DOC (SEWING UP MY KNEE) AND ONE OF THE PHYSIOS"

29 LIVERPOOL 0 — MANCHESTER UNITED 1

FA PREMIERSHIP

DATE: Saturday March 3

ATTENDANCE: 44,403 (Anfield)

REFEREE: Martin Atkinson

GOAL: 90 MINS (0-1) O'SHEA - Ronaldo's free kick, awarded for Steve Finnan's foul on Giggs, was only parried by goalkeeper PepeReina and O'Shea shot the ball home.

THE GAME: Manchester United grabbed a dramatic last-minute victory at Anfield to maintain their six-point lead at the top of the Premiership. However, this victory was not achieved without casualties. Rooney was forced off through injury suffering a gashed knee from a Jamie Carragher tackle that earned the Liverpool man a booking in the 73rd minute. Scholes was sent off for throwing a punch at, but not connecting with, Xabi Alonso in the 86th minute. Those events aside, it was a close-fought and exciting encounter that was decided by Rooney's replacement O'Shea – who thumped his shot into the roof of the net for a late, late winner.

JOHN O'SHEA: "That must have been soul-destroying for Chelsea. With a couple of minutes to go they were probably thinking we would drop two points, or even three, because we were down to ten men. Instead, we scored and the gap is still there at the top of the table."

SIR ALEX FERGUSON: "You need that bit of luck to win a championship. Liverpool played well today and their pressing game upset us. I think they were very unlucky, but that's football."

RAFA BENITEZ: "It's difficult to explain how we lost, we had attacks, corners and free-kicks, whereas they were not doing that much attacking."

DIRK KUYT: "Manchester United have got five or six match winners and you can't deny they will be worthy champions."

LIVERPOOL	MANCHESTER UNITED
Reina	Van der Sar
Finnan	Neville
Carragher	Vidic
Agger	Ferdinand
Riise	Evra
Gerrard	*Subbed 63 mins (Silvestre)*
Alonso	Ronaldo
Gerrard	Scholes
Sissoko	Carrick
Subbed 79 mins (Crouch)	Giggs
Gonzalez	Rooney
Subbed 60 mins (Aurelio)	*Subbed 73 mins (O'Shea)*
Kuyt	Larsson
Bellamy	*Subbed 67 mins (Saha)*
Subbed 69 mins (Pennant)	*sub: Silvestre*
sub: Crouch	*sub: O'Shea*
sub: Aurelio	*sub: Saha*
sub: Pennant	**Subs not used:** Kuszczak, Brown
Subs not used: Dudek, Hyppia	
Coach: *Rafa Benitez*	**Coach:** *Sir Alex Ferguson*

30 MANCHESTER UNITED 4 — BOLTON WANDERERS 1

FA PREMIERSHIP

DATE: Saturday March 17

ATTENDANCE: 76,058 (Old Trafford)

REFEREE: Alan Wiley

GOALS: 14 MINS (1-0) PARK - Ronaldo, on the left, headed the ball forward and chased it into the area. He then cut inside to pull the ball back from the byline inside the six-yard box, for the unmarked Park to shoot home right-footed from ten yards; **17 MINS (2-0) ROONEY** - Ronaldo and Rooney combined to clear Ivan Campo's throw-in with a one-two. Ronaldo raced up field before feeding the ball to his left for Rooney, on the edge of the Bolton area, to score with an exquisite chip over the advancing Jaaskelainen and into the net; **25 MINS (3-0) PARK** - cut in from the right on a parallel run with the area before laying a pass off for Ronaldo. Ronaldo's fancy footwork mesmerised the Bolton defence before he unleashed a low shot from the edge of the area that Jaaskelainen dived towards his right post to save. But the ball spun away from him and Park raced in to net it in the opposite corner; **74 MINS (4-0) ROONEY** - chased Alan Smith's long ball and brought it under control before firing an angled right foot shot into the far corner of the net; **87 MINS (4-1) SPEED** - Penalty. Converted by veteran midfielder Gary with a shot down the middle. Awarded after Vidic had fouled Abdoulaye Faye.

THE GAME: Manchester United – without the injured Fletcher (ankle), Saha (hamstring), Silvestre (shoulder), Solskjaer (knee), Van der Sar (calf) and the suspended Scholes – overcame the early set-back of losing captain Neville through injury after ten minutes by sewing up the match over the next fifteen! Rooney's 50th goal for United was sandwiched between a brace from Park, in for the departed Henrik Larsson, to attain an unbeatable 3-0 lead. Rooney added a fourth goal in the second-half after taking over the captaincy after 56 minutes following the substitution of Giggs – who had previously taken the captain's armband from the injured Neville. The United players wore black armbands in a tribute to the club's 92-year-old tea lady Nesta Burgess, who had died during the week.

SIR ALEX FERGUSON: "The combination between Ronaldo and Rooney for the second goal was tremendous, the weight of the pass was perfect, but that's what he's all about."

RONALDO: "The confidence in the team is very high at the moment. We finished the game in the first-half and that's good because we have another game in two days. There's no time to rest, but England is like that. You need to keep going and keep winning."

MANCHESTER UNITED	BOLTON WANDERERS
Kuszczak	Jaaskelainen
Neville	Hunt
Subbed 10 mins (Brown)	Faye
Ferdinand	Ben Haim
Vidic	Gardner
Heinze	Nolan
Ronaldo	Campo
Subbed 70 mins (Smith)	*Subbed 78 mins (Thompson)*
Carrick	Speed
O'Shea	Davies
Park	*Subbed 52 mins (Andranik)*
Giggs	Anelka
Subbed 56 mins (Richardson)	Pedersen
Rooney	*Subbed 28 mins (Diouf)*
sub: Brown	*sub: Thompson*
sub: Smith	*sub: Andranik*
sub: Richardson	*sub: Diouf*
Subs not used: Evra, Heaton	**Subs not used:** Stelios, Walker
Coach: *Sir Alex Ferguson*	**Coach:** *Sam Allardyce*

31 MANCHESTER UNITED 4 — BLACKBURN ROVERS 1

FA PREMIERSHIP

DATE: Saturday March 31

ATTENDANCE: 76,098 (Old Trafford)

REFEREE: Chris Foy

GOALS: 29 MINS (0-1) DERBYSHIRE - Benny McCarthy and Morten Gamst Pedersen combined on the left allowing the latter to hit a near-post cross, which Carrick narrowly failed to cut out and Van der Sar failed to hold. This allowed Matt Derbyshire to score from close range; **61 MINS (1-1) SCHOLES** - pounced on a loose ball on the edge of the area which Chris Samba was unable to control. Scholes skipped past two challenges before firing a low angled shot from 14 yards into the net; **73 MINS (2-1) CARRICK** - Ronaldo played a one-two with Heinze from a left-wing corner before cutting inside, skipping past Ryan Nelson and pulling the ball back from the byline. The ball ran through a crowd of players to beyond the far post where Carrick drilled home an angled shot from ten yards; **83 MINS (3-1) PARK** - was the first to react after Ronaldo's 19-yard free kick had been parried by Friedel and side-footed his volley home from six yards out; **90 MINS (4-1) SOLSKJAER** - Park picked up a wayward pass and released Rooney down the left and the England forward turned and headed for goal but was tackled. Park followed up and clipped the ball across goal which Rooney narrowly missed and Solskjaer swept home side-footed at the far post.

THE GAME: A stunning second-half performance saw United overcome a one-goal first-half deficit and the loss of Nemanja Vidic who was stretchered off with a shoulder injury. United had squandered chances through their own poor finishing and the Blackburn's defence willingness to get in the way of anything remotely dangerous from the home side. After the break, United playing superb football exploited Blackburn's errors as possession and free kicks were conceded in dangerous areas and crosses were not cleared - all of which led to United's four goals.

SIR ALEX FERGUSON: "The second-half performance was our best of the season. It was the kind of performance you would expect from a championship team."

MARK HUGHES: "United won't be denied now. In fact I think they will win it comfortably."

MANCHESTER UNITED	BLACKBURN ROVERS
Van der Sar	Friedel
Brown	Emerton
Ferdinand	Samba
Vidic	Nelsen
Subbed 28 mins (O'Shea)	Warnock
Heinze	Dunn
Park	Mokoena
Carrick	Tugay
Scholes	*Subbed 74 mins (Peter)*
Ronaldo	Pedersen
Subbed 84 mins (Solskjaer)	McCarthy
Giggs	*Subbed 69 mins (Roberts)*
Subbed 84 mins (Smith)	Derbyshire
Rooney	*sub: Peter*
sub: O'Shea	*sub: Roberts*
sub: Solskjaer	**Subs not used:** Nonda, Enckelman, Henchoz
sub: Smith	**Coach:** *Mark Hughes*
Subs not used: Richardson, Kuszczak	
Coach: *Sir Alex Ferguson*	

32
PORTSMOUTH 2
MANCHESTER UNITED 1

FA PREMIERSHIP

DATE: Saturday April 7

ATTENDANCE: 20,233 (Fratton Park)

REFEREE: Mark Clattenburg

GOALS: 30 MINS (1-0) TAYLOR - Gary O'Neil dispossessed Richardson and the ball ran to Benjani, who unleashed a first-time, right-foot shot from 22 yards which Van der Sar parried. But Matty Taylor beat Ferdinand to the rebound to knock the ball home; **89 MINS (2-0) FERDINAND OWN GOAL** – Ferdinand cut out Taylor's cross intended for LuaLua but the pass-back to his goalkeeper left Van der Sar stranded and the ball ended up in the net; **89 MINS (2-1) O'SHEA** - goalkeeper David James was unable to hold Solskjaer's shot through a defender's legs from just inside the area, allowing O'Shea to pounce on the loose ball and knock it into the net from close range.

THE GAME: The six-point lead Manchester United held at the top of the Premiership since Boxing Day was halved following this defeat at Fratton Park, and Chelsea's 1-0 win over Tottenham. Portsmouth started confidently and in James they had a goalkeeper bidding to create a new Premiership clean-sheets record which was to be cruelly denied him by O'Shea's late consolation goal. United did have spells of playing good football but they were ultimately undone by goalkeeping and defensive errors. Ferdinand failed to stop Taylor after Van der Sar did not hold O'Neil's shot in the first-half. Then, near the end, it was Ferdinand who put through his own net – following a mix-up with his keeper – and the points were conceded to Portsmouth.

HARRY REDKNAPP: "You've still got to fancy United. They've got a better run-in, they've got three points in hand and a better goal difference."

DAVID JAMES: "Chelsea will fancy their chances now, especially as they still have to play United - and with their scabby 1-0 wins, they could do it. United are all about goals and fantastic displays, but Chelsea keep grinding out results and arguably that's the mark of champions. That's the way they are doing it. As a fan I would rather see United win it."

SIR ALEX FERGUSON: "I won't complain about losing to Portsmouth. The main thing now is to recover and show our mettle."

PORTSMOUTH	MANCHESTER UNITED
James	Van der Sar
Lauren	O'Shea
Primus	Ferdinand OG
Stefanovic	Brown
Traore	Heinze
O'Neil	Fletcher
	Subbed 59 mins (Solskjaer)
Davis	Carrick
Hughes	*Subbed 77 mins (Smith)*
Taylor	Scholes
Benjani	Ronaldo
Subbed 67 mins (Lualua)	Rooney
Kanu	Richardson
Subbed 81 mins (Kranjcar)	*Subbed HT (Giggs)*
sub: Lualua	*sub: Solskjaer*
sub: Kranjcar	*sub: Smith*
Subs not used: Ashdown, Todorov, Pamarot	*sub: Giggs*
Coach: Harry Redknapp	**Subs not used:** Evra, Kuszczak
	Coach: Sir Alex Ferguson

You don't see many of these in a season: John O'Shea nets a late, late winner against Liverpool

33
MANCHESTER UNITED 2
SHEFFIELD UNITED 0

FA PREMIERSHIP

DATE: Tuesday April 17

ATTENDANCE: 75,540 (Old Trafford)

REFEREE: Rob Styles

GOALS: 4 MINS (1-0) CARRICK - Ronaldo slipped the ball into the path of Carrick in the right channel inside the area, and he chipped the ball over the advancing goalkeeper Paddy Kenny and into the net; **50 MINS (2-0) ROONEY** - escaped Blades full-back Rob Kozluk and ran behind Chris Morgan to latch on to a Giggs superb long floated pass. Rooney took one touch before thumping the ball home with a right-foot angled shot from ten yards out.

THE GAME: Giggs made his 500th Lague appearance for Manchester United as the Premiership leaders did not need to overstretch themselves to beat relegation-threatened Sheffield United with a goal early in each half. Carrick scored his fourth goal in three home matches while Rooney, as dangerous as ever, scored his 20th goal of the season. United dominated possession and territory and at times played with just Brown and Heinze at the back – such was their control of the match. It was their tenth successive Premiership win at Old Trafford as the title loomed ever closer.

RYAN GIGGS: "At 1-0 you're never comfortable... so seeing that second goal go in we could relax a little bit more and keep the ball."

SIR ALEX FERGUSON: "The second goal was a marvellous strike. It was a pleasing result and the performance was economical. We didn't kill ourselves which is important."

GARY NEVILLE: "It is a great prospect knowing we are going into the last month still going for three major trophies. It is where we have wanted to be for three seasons. Now we are going to enjoy it."

MANCHESTER UNITED	SHEFFIELD UNITED
Kuszczak	Kenny
Fletcher	Geary
Brown	Kozluk
Heinze	*Subbed 77 mins (Armstrong)*
Evra	Jagielka
Subbed 21 mins (Richardson)	Morgan
Ronaldo	Kilgallon
Carrick	Webber
Scholes	Montgomery
Rooney	Tonge
Smith	Kazim-Richards
Giggs	*Subbed 75 mins (Gillespie)*
Subbed 80 mins (Solskjaer)	Shelton
sub: Richardson	*Subbed 89 mins (Nade)*
sub: Solskjaer	*sub: Armstrong*
Subs not used: Van der Sar, O'Shea, Cathcart	*sub: Gillespie*
Coach: Sir Alex Ferguson	*sub: Nade*
	Subs not used: A Quinn, Fathi
	Coach: Neil Warnock

"EVERYBODY WAS HOPING HAITCH WOULD STAY ON. ME AND RIO BOTH TALKED TO HIM, TRYING TO PERSUADE HIM, BUT WITH NO LUCK. HE HAD PROMISED HELSINBORGS, HIS CLUB IN SWEDEN, THAT HE WOULD RETURN FOR THE START OF THEIR SEASON AND HE'D ALSO PROMISED HIS FAMILY. SO HE WENT BACK AS ARRANGED IN THE MIDDLE OF MARCH"

34 — MANCHESTER UNITED 1 / MIDDLESBROUGH 1

FA PREMIERSHIP

DATE: Saturday April 21

ATTENDANCE: 75,967 (Old Trafford)

REFEREE: Peter Walton

GOALS: 3 MINS (1-0) RICHARDSON - Rooney chased a cross-field pass from Scholes. He chested down and took it into the area. He then dragged the ball away from the advancing goalkeeper and Richardson darted alongside Rooney to knock the ball into the unguarded net; 45 MINS (1-1) VIDUKA - Aussie Mark scored with a diving header from a Stewart Downing left-wing cross which the injured Ferdinand was unable to deal with.

THE GAME: Middlesbrough tested and stretched Manchester United and earned a deserved point. United had made more chances but, aside from Richardson's first goal of the season, only one other effort was on target. In truth United were not at their best and the loss through injury of Ferdinand seemed the bigger blow, particularly with Neville, Silvestre and Vidic all still out of action. The one silver lining for United was that Chelsea did not exploit the dropping of points by managing only a goalless draw with Newcastle the following day.

SIR ALEX FERGUSON: "The injuries have killed us... we were over over-anxious, rushing our passes when we needed some calm... Rio's injury was the biggest blow. We mustn't feel sorry for ourselves. It is time to show what Manchester United and the players are made of."

MANCHESTER UNITED	MIDDLESBROUGH
Van der Sar	Schwarzer
O'Shea	Davies
Brown	Woodgate
Ferdinand	Pogatetz
Subbed 46 (Giggs)	Taylor
Heinze	Cattermole
Ronaldo	Boateng
Carrick	Rochemback
Scholes	Downing
Richardson	Viduka
Subbed 46 (Fletcher)	Yakubu
Rooney	*Subbed 81 mins (Lee)*
Smith	*sub: Lee*
Subbed 67 mins (Solskjaer)	
sub: Fletcher	*Subs not used: Jones, Huth, Morrison, Johnson*
sub: Solskjaer	*Coach: Gareth Southgate*
sub: Giggs	
Subs not used: Kuszczak, Eagles	
Coach: Sir Alex Ferguson	

---

35 — EVERTON 2 / MANCHESTER UNITED 4

FA PREMIERSHIP

DATE: Saturday April 28

ATTENDANCE: 39,682 (Goodison Park)

REFEREE: Alan Wiley

GOALS: 12 MINS (1-0) STUBBS - Defender Alan fired home a 30-yard free kick which deflected off Carrick's foot and beyond the already committed Van der Sar into the net; 50 MINS (2-0) FERNANDES - Mikel Arteta, on the halfway line, slipped the ball through to Mani Fernandes, who finished his run with a rising right-foot shot from edge of the area and into the top right-hand corner of the net; 61 MINS (2-1) O'SHEA - goalkeeper Iain Turner went to collect but, under no pressure, dropped a Giggs left-wing corner and O'Shea hooked it home from five yards; 68 MINS (2-2) P NEVILLE OWN GOAL - Ronaldo produced a downward header that hit the goalkeeper's feet from Carrick's left-wing corner. Phil Neville attempted to clear the loose ball but put it into his own net; 79 MINS (2-3) ROONEY - Ronaldo intercepted Tony Hibbert's diagonal pass and played it out to the right for O'Shea to centre. Lee Carsley got in a glancing header but directed it across goal where Rooney was waiting to bring it under control. He avoided Hibbert's sliding tackle and slipped it past the goalkeeper into the right hand corner of the net; 90 MINS (2-4) EAGLES - Rooney, in the third minute of stoppage time, turned and slipped the ball into space for Chris Eagles to score with a curling right foot shot.

THE GAME: After five minutes of the second-half Manchester United trailed Everton 2-0 while at Stamford Bridge Chelsea led Bolton 2-1. For the first time, the two were separated only by United's goal difference and the tide looked to be turning in Chelsea's favour... but then it all changed. Bolton equalised, giving United a reduced two-point advantage and then United gave a devastating play of superlative football with Rooney and Giggs outstanding. In the last half an hour, Manchester United turned a two-goal deficit into a 4-2 victory, creating a host of chances from which their goals were reaped. With 11 minutes remaining, Rooney gave United the lead and as the match went into stoppage time the news filtered through that Bolton had held Chelsea. To cap off the afternoon's celebrations, Eagles added a fourth goal. Manchester United now moved five points clear of their nearest rivals with three games to go.

---

36 — MANCHESTER CITY 0 / MANCHESTER UNITED 1

FA PREMIERSHIP

DATE: Saturday May 5

ATTENDANCE: 47,244 (City of Manchester Stadium)

REFEREE: Rob Styles

GOAL: 34 MINS (0-1) RONALDO - Penalty. Sent goalkeeper the wrong way from the spot kick after he had been brought down by Michael Ball.

THE GAME: Not the greatest Manchester derby that has ever been. United controlled the match with City defending in depth, which ended up making it a very ordinary game. The opening was marred by Ball's deliberate stamp on Ronaldo, the newly- elected PFA Player and Young Player of the Year, halfway inside the United half. Neither referee or his assistants saw the incident but TV did. Later Ball admitted the resulting FA charge of violent conduct and he also sent a personal apology to Ronaldo. The match was decided by the same two players with Ball conceding the decisive penalty from which Ronaldo scored his 17th Premiership goal of the season. The result left Chelsea having to win the following day at Arsenal – they didn't and Manchester United were confirmed the Premiership champions for the first time in four years and Rooney gained his first Premiership medal.

SIR ALEX FERGUSON: "What you saw today is human courage. After the result in midweek, they showed fantastic courage and just got on with it. You didn't see the best of Manchester United because there was a lot of tiredness out there, but they did the job."

STUART PEARCE: "The result here finishes the title race. United will be worthy champions; they are a very good team. So are Chelsea, of course, but whoever finishes on top of the league after 38 games deserves to."

MANCHESTER CITY	MANCHESTER UNITED
Isaksson	Van der Sar
Onuoha	Brown
Dunne	Ferdinand
Distin	Vidic
Ball	Heinze
Vassell	Ronaldo
Hamann	Carrick
Subbed HT (Sun Jihai)	Giggs
Johnson	Scholes
Ireland	Rooney
Subbed 69 mins (Dickov)	*Subbed 87 mins (O'Shea)*
Beasley	Smith
Subbed 61 mins (Sinclair)	*Subbed 73 mins (Fletcher)*
Mpenza	*sub: O'Shea*
sub: Sun Jihai	*sub: Fletcher*
sub: Dickov	*Subs not used: Kuszczak,*
sub: Sinclair	*Solskjaer, Richardson*
Subs not used: Weaver, Samaras	*Coach: Sir Alex Ferguson*
Coach: Stuart Pearce	

SIR ALEX FERGUSON: "We have a five-point lead and a superior goal difference, giving us a marvellous chancer with three games left. But the most important thing is that my lads are having a real go. If you do that, and with the finishers we have in our side, we are always likely to score. This result is very significant."

JOSE MOURINHO: "Mathematically there is a chance, and when the chance is still there you have to believe and chase it. They have to lose two matches and Chelsea have to win all three. United will feel under no pressure now."

WAYNE ROONEY: "According to a few people I have been suffering a goal drought all season. In fact, I have bettered last season's tally already and that of the season before. I'm feeling good and hopefully that can continue. We play to the end. You've seen Chelsea do the same. It is a good battle between us..."

PHIL NEVILLE: "I said to Scholesy he was a jammy so-and-so and he thanked me for the goal. We're the best of friends. He was asking why I didn't shake his hand after the game, but I was too gutted. I congratulated him for winning the league."

EVERTON	MANCHESTER UNITED
Turner	Van der Sar
Hibbert	O'Shea
Yobo	Heinze
Stubbs	Brown
Lescott	Evra
Arteta	*Subbed 55 mins (Richardson)*
P Neville OG	Carrick
Carsley	Scholes
Subbed 84 mins (Van der Meyde)	Solskjaer
Fernandes	*Subbed 87 mins (Eagles)*
Osman	Giggs
Subbed 72 mins (McFadden)	Rooney
Vaughan	Smith
Subbed 71 mins (Beattie)	*Subbed 62 mins (Ronaldo)*
sub: Van der Meyde	*sub: Richardson*
sub: McFadden	*sub: Eagles*
sub: Beattie	*sub: Ronaldo*
Subs not used: Wright, Naysmith	*Subs not used: Kuszczak, Lee*
Coach: David Moyes	*Coach: Sir Alex Ferguson*

37
CHELSEA 0
MANCHESTER UNITED 0

FA PREMIERSHIP

DATE: Wednesday May 11

ATTENDANCE: 41,794 (Stamford Bridge)

REFEREE: Graham Poll

THE GAME: Manchester United's first match since taking the crown from Chelsea inevitably was at Stamford Bridge. Both Ferguson and Jose Mourinho decided to rest many of their leading names. The match itself turned out to be bad-tempered reserve game with six bookings and Mourinho mistakenly believed he had been sent from the dug-out by referee Poll. The best chance of the match fell to Chelsea in the final minute when United's Kieran Lee needed to clear Ben Sahar's shot off line.

SIR ALEX FERGUSON: "In the last two years Chelsea have dominated the Premier League and we had a big job to catch them. The key to it was getting a good start to the season and I think we did that really well. The start gave us the momentum and from that moment on I don't think we ever lost it. That wasn't easy, keeping a lead in the Premier League for six months, with Chelsea on our coat-tails."

CHELSEA	MANCHESTER UNITED
Cudicini	Kuszczak
Ferreira	Lee
Terry	Brown
Essien	O'Shea
Bridge	Heinze
Diarra	*Subbed 66 mins (Carrick)*
Subbed 88 mins (Morais)	Smith
Makelele	Fletcher
Mikel	Richardson
Subbed 45 mins (J Cole)	Eagles
Wright-Phillips	Dong
Kalou	*Subbed 73 mins (Rooney)*
Sinclair	Solskjaer
Subbed 55 mins (Sahar)	*sub: Carrick*
sub: Morais	*sub: Rooney*
sub: J Cole	**Subs not used:** *Van der Sar, Ferdinand, Scholes*
sub: Sahar	
Subs not used: *Hilario, Geremi*	**Coach:** *Sir Alex Ferguson*
Coach: *Jose Mourinho*	

38
MANCHESTER UNITED 0
WEST HAM UNITED 1

FA PREMIERSHIP

DATE: Sunday May 13

ATTENDANCE: 75,927 (Old Trafford)

REFEREE: Martin Atkinson

GOAL: 45 MINS (0-1) TEVEZ - Hammers striker Bobby Zamora beat Heinze in the air from Robert Green's drop kick. The ball fell to Carlos Tevez, who held off Carrick before exchanging passes with Zamora. The Argentine then got past Brown as the ball ricocheted in the air and he placed his effort past Van der Sar.

THE GAME: Neville and Giggs finally lifted the Premiership trophy. There was other silverware too for Sir Alex Ferguson as Barclays Manger of the Season; for Ronaldo as Barclays Player of the Season (to join with his PFA Player of the Year and Young Player of the Year Awards) and a Merit Award to Ryan Giggs for winning his record-breaking ninth championship medal. The game itself was all about West Ham's fight for survival and the need for a point. A Tevez goal on the stroke of half-time decided the game – giving them the double over Manchester United – and kept Hammers up and so everyone was happy!

GARY NEVILLE: "It's been so long since we've won it. I think for many years we thought it was our right to win it year in, year out and we've found out in the last three or four years how difficult it is. We're delighted how we've performed this season. It has been a real team effort."

MANCHESTER UNITED	WEST HAM UNITED
Van der Sar	Green
O'Shea	Neill
Brown	Ferdinand
Heinze	Collins
Evra	McCartney
Subbed 57 mins (Giggs)	*Subbed 28 mins (Spector)*
Solskjaer	Benayoun
Carrick	Noble
Subbed 58 mins (Scholes)	Reo-Coker
Fletcher	Boa Morte
Richardson	Tevez ⚽
Rooney	*Subbed 82 mins (Mullins)*
Smith	Zamora
Subbed 58 mins (Ronaldo)	*Subbed 63 mins (Harewood)*
sub: Giggs	*sub: Spector*
sub: Scholes	*sub: Mullins*
sub: Ronaldo	*sub: Harewood*
Subs not used: *Kuszczak, Vidic*	**Subs not used:** *Walker, Davenport*
Coach: *Sir Alex Ferguson*	**Coach:** *Alan Curbishley*

3 MINS (1-0) RICHARDSON - ROONEY CHASED A CROSS-FIELD PASS FROM SCHOLES. HE CHESTED DOWN AND TOOK IT INTO THE AREA. HE THEN DRAGGED THE BALL AWAY FROM THE ADVANCING GOALKEEPER AND RICHARDSON DARTED ALONGSIDE ROONEY TO KNOCK THE BALL INTO THE UNGUARDED NET.

34 MINS (0-1) RONALDO - PENALTY. SENT GOALKEEPER THE WRONG WAY FROM THE SPOT KICK AFTER HE HAD BEEN BROUGHT DOWN BY BALL.

61 MINS (2-1) O'SHEA - GOALKEEPER IAIN TURNER WENT TO COLLECT BUT, UNDER NO PRESSURE, DROPPED A GIGGS LEFT-WING CORNER AND O'SHEA HOOKED IT HOME FROM FIVE YARDS.

FA CUP

MANCHESTER UNITED IN THE FA CUP

39

MANCHESTER UNITED 2
ASTON VILLA 1

FA CUP THIRD ROUND

DATE: Sunday January 7

ATTENDANCE: 74,924 (Old Trafford)

REFEREE: Martin Atkinson

GOALS: 55 MINS (1-0) LARSSON - a Rooney square pass set up Larsson to fire into the top right-hand corner of the net from 12 yards; **74 MINS (1-1) BAROS** - United failed to fully clear a corner and Cahill's attempted shot bobbled back into the area to Milan Baros who shot right-footed from 12 yards inside the left post; **90 MINS (2-1) SOLSKJAER** - Evra regained possession for United just outside the centre circle in the Villa half and released the ball to the forward-running Ronaldo. He played a one-touch pass to Rooney who in turn played a diagonal pass to Solskjaer on the edge of the Villa penalty area. Solskjaer drilled a low angled first time hit shot that went under goalkeeper Kiraly and into the net.

THE GAME: Solskjaer scored a dramatic stoppage-time winner to put Manchester United into the fourth round. It was what United deserved after Larsson, making his debut on loan from Helsingborgs, had put United ahead in the 55th minute. His instinctive half-volley lifted the Old Trafford crowd – however, a Baros equaliser looked set to force the tie into a replay until supersub Solskjaer struck.

MARTIN O'NEILL: "We're all disappointed but Gabor is distraught."

SIR ALEX FERGUSON: "I think we deserved to go through because the number of chances we created was terrific. I was thinking about it being a replay... but with Ole on the pitch you know you've always got a chance of scoring."

MANCHESTER UNITED	ASTON VILLA
Kuszczak	Kiraly
Neville	Hughes
Ferdinand	Ridgewell
Brown	Cahill
Evra	Bouma
Ronaldo	McCann
Carrick	Osbourne
Subbed 89 mins (O'Shea)	Petrov
Giggs	*Subbed 66 mins (Samuel)*
Park	Barry
Subbed 72 mins (Fletcher)	Agbonlahor
Larsson ⚽	Angel
Subbed 78 mins (Solskjaer)	*Subbed 53 mins (Baros)*
Rooney	*sub: Samuel*
sub: O'Shea	*sub: Baros* ⚽
sub: Fletcher	*Subs not used: Davis,*
sub: Solskjaer ⚽	*Whittingham, Olejnik*
Subs not used: Van der Sar,	*Coach: Martin O'Neill*
Heinze	
Coach: Sir Alex Ferguson	

40

MANCHESTER UNITED 2
PORTSMOUTH 1

FA CUP FOURTH ROUND

DATE: Saturday January 27

ATTENDANCE: 71,137 (Old Trafford)

REFEREE: Mike Riley

GOALS: 77 MINS (1-0) ROONEY - Carrick dispossessed Gary O'Neil and instigated a move involving Larsson, with a pass, Giggs, with a cross, and Rooney, with a tap into an empty net from six yards out; **83 MINS (2-0) ROONEY** - at inside-right position, scored with a fantastic floated chipped effort that sailed over David James and into the net; **87 MINS (2-1) KANU** - Pedro Mendes's drive into a crowded penalty area was deflected by Kanu into the net, leaving Kuszczak wrong-footed.

THE GAME: It was hard work and it needed a goalscoring, match-winning substitute appearance from Rooney to help Manchester United book their place in the fifth round. The hosts had found it hard to break down a resolute Portsmouth side although they did have two perfectly legitimate goals disallowed. Firstly, Vidic saw his effort cleared from behind the goal-line by Pompey midfielder Mendes, while Larsson also had the ball in the net but was ruled to be offside. The arrival of Rooney for Solskjaer on the hour made the difference with two goals in a six-minute spell – the first a simple tap-in and the second a spectacular chipped effort. Kanu scored a consolation and caused the last few minutes to be anxious ones for United, but the home side held on.

SIR ALEX FERGUSON: "He [Rooney] just had the vision and audacity to do that. The boy has got the kind of courage to do that, to try things. He has always had that."

RIO FERDINAND: "During this spell, when people have been questioning his goalscoring, Wayne's work-rate and team ethic never wavered at all. He's a joy to play with and watch."

WAYNE ROONEY: "In a way I am more pleased with the first one than the second as I need to score the easier ones."

MANCHESTER UNITED	PORTSMOUTH
Kuszczak	James
Neville	Lauren
Vidic	Campbell
Ferdinand	Primus
Evra	Johnson
Park	Hughes
Carrick	*Subbed 82 mins (Douala)*
Scholes	Taylor
Giggs	O'Neil
Subbed 85 mins (Fletcher)	Mendes
Larsson	Kranjcar
Solskjaer	*Subbed 80 mins (Mwaruwari)*
Subbed 60 mins (Rooney)	Cole
sub: Fletcher	*Subbed 62 mins (Kanu)*
sub: Rooney ⚽⚽	*sub: Douala*
Subs not used: Van der Sar,	*sub: Mwaruwari*
O'Shea, Silvestre	*sub: Kanu*
Coach: Sir Alex Ferguson	*Subs not used: Ashdown,*
	Thompson
	Coach: Harry Redknapp

41

MANCHESTER UNITED 1
READING 1

FA CUP FIFTH ROUND

DATE: Saturday February 17

ATTENDANCE: 70,608 (Old Trafford)

REFEREE: Graham Poll

GOALS: 45 MINS (1-0) CARRICK - Ronaldo cut in from the left and played the ball off to Carrick, who unleashed a first-time 25-yard shot that squeezed between goalkeeper Adam Federici and the left post; **67 MINS (1-1) GUNNARSSON** - midfielder Brynjar equalised with a header from 10 yards out from a right-wing corner.

THE GAME: Reading made seven changes – citing the fight for a UEFA Cup place more important – and Manchester United made six changes – with an upcoming Champions League tie the following week – to their respective sides, but still produced a competitive cup-tie. However, it was United who rued missing a whole host of goalscoring opportunities, although Solskjaer did have the ball in the net but was (wrongly) adjudged to have been offside. Michael Carrick gave United the lead on the stroke of half-time but Reading did not crumble and tenaciously fought back to earn a replay courtesy of Brynjar Gunnarsson's equaliser.

SIR ALEX FERGUSON: "It was a good team performance and we deserved to win, but we just couldn't take the chances that we had."

MANCHESTER UNITED	READING
Kuszczak	Federici
Brown	Gunnarsson ⚽
Vidic	Bikey
Silvestre	Ingimarsson
Heinze	De La Cruz
Subbed 73 mins (Evra)	Shorey
Park	Sidwell
Subbed 73 mins (Scholes)	Oster
Fletcher	*Subbed 86 mins (Sodje)*
Ronaldo	Convey
Carrick ⚽	*Subbed 71 mins (Hunt)*
Saha	Seol
Solskjaer	*Subbed 89 mins (Little)*
Subbed 73 mins (Larsson)	Kitson
sub: Evra	*sub: Sodje*
sub: Scholes	*sub: Hunt*
sub: Larsson	*sub: Little*
Subs not used: Heaton,	*Subs not used: Hahnemann,*
O'Shea	*Lita*
Coach: Sir Alex Ferguson	*Coach: Steve Coppell*

Gabriel Heinze scores United's first goal during the FA Cup fifth round replay against plucky Reading

6 MINS (0-3) SOLSKJAER - CHASED DOWN RONALDO'S SUPERLATIVE PASS AND HAD TIME AND SPACE TO SHOOT PAST FEDERICI WITH THE OUTSIDE OF HIS RIGHT FOOT.

2 MINS (0-1) HEINZE - O'SHEA CUT IN FROM THE RIGHT AND PULLED THE BALL BACK FROM THE BYLINE BUT RICHARDSON COMPLETELY MISSED HIS KICK. THE BALL ROLLED OUT OF THE AREA WHERE HEINZE FIRED IN A POWERFUL LEFT-FOOT SHOT WHICH GOALKEEPER FEDERICI WAS UNABLE TO HOLD — THE BALL ROLLED INTO THE NET.

45 MINS (1-0) CARRICK - RONALDO CUT IN FROM THE LEFT AND PLAYED THE BALL OFF TO CARRICK WHO UNLEASHED A FIRST-TIME HIT 25-YARD SHOT THAT SQUEEZED IN BETWEEN GOALKEEPER ADAM FEDERICI AND THE LEFT POST.

42
READING 2
MANCHESTER UNITED 3

FA CUP FIFTH ROUND REPLAY

DATE: Tuesday February 27

ATTENDANCE: 23,821 (Madjeski Stadium)

REFEREE: Howard Webb

GOALS: 2 MINS (0-1) HEINZE - O'Shea cut in from the right and pulled the ball back from the byline but Richardson completely missed his kick. The ball rolled out of the area where Heinze fired in a powerful left-foot shot which goalkeeper Federici was unable to hold – the ball rolled into the net; **4 MINS (0-2) SAHA** - just outside the Reading area on the left, he chested down a superb diagonal cross-field pass from Neville before firing home an angled left-foot shot inside the far post from ten yards; **6 MINS (0-3) SOLSKJAER** - chased down Ronaldo's superlative pass and had time and space to shoot past Federici with the outside of his right foot; **23 MINS (1-3) KITSON** - John Oster's right-wing corner was flicked on at the near post by Ingimarsson for the unmarked Kitson to score from close range at the far post; **84 MINS (2-3) LITA** - striker Leroy headed home Ulises De La Cruz's right-wing cross into the net.

THE GAME: Manchester United looked set to have comfortably booked their quarter-final place by racing into a 3-0 lead by the sixth minute. Fortunately for Reading the potential embarrassing onslaught did not continue and as United took their foot off the accelerator, the Royals studiously began an amazing fight-back. There was little concern about Kitson's goal midway through the first-half but United were put in a defensive frenzy when Lita made 3-2 with six minutes remaining - and United knew a lot could happen in just six minutes! Reading put United under pressure and almost pulled it off when Brynjar Gunnarsson hit the crossbar in stoppage time. United held on but only just.

SIR ALEX FERGUSON: "We rode our luck. There's no doubt about that because Reading pummelled us in the second-half. It was an incredible tie and I thought it was heading into extra-time because we lost the momentum when Reading scored their second goal."

READING		MANCHESTER UNITED	
Federici		Van der Sar	
De La Cruz		Silvestre	
Gunnarsson		Brown	
Bikey		Ferdinand	
Ingimarsson		Heinze	⚽
Shorey		Park	
Seol		Fletcher	
Subbed 68 mins (Little)		O'Shea	
Sidwell		Richardson	
Oster		Saha	⚽
Kitson	⚽	*Subbed 76 mins (Rooney)*	
Doyle		Solskjaer	⚽
Subbed 71 mins (Lita)		*Subbed 89 mins (Ronaldo)*	
sub: Little		*sub: Rooney*	
sub: Lita	⚽	*sub: Ronaldo*	
Subs not used: Hahnemann, Hunt, Sodje		*Subs not used: Kuszczak, Smith, Scholes*	
Coach: Steve Coppell		**Coach: Sir Alex Ferguson**	

43
MIDDLESBROUGH 2
MANCHESTER UNITED 2

FA CUP QUARTER-FINAL

DATE: Saturday March 10

ATTENDANCE: 33,308 (Riverside Stadium)

REFEREE: Rob Styles

GOALS: 23 MINS (0-1) ROONEY - latched on to a Giggs pass on the edge of the area and despatched a low right-foot shot into the left corner of the net; **45 MINS (1-1) CATTERMOLE** - Boro youngster Lee, with his back to goal, received a headed pass from Julio Arca. He took one touch and then hit a half-volley into the net from eight yards; **47 MINS (2-1) BOATENG** - unmarked Dutchman George headed home at the far post from Stewart Downing's right-wing corner; **68 MINS (2-2) RONALDO** - Penalty. Fired home to the left after Boateng was penalised for handball.

THE GAME: Middlesbrough were unchanged for the first time since December while Manchester United fielded their strongest available side for the first time in the competition despite the loss of goalkeeper Edwin van der Sar with a calf injury just before what turned out to be a thrilling cup-tie. Both sides led during the game with United's first-half lead established by Rooney cancelled out and overtaken by goals by Cattermole and Boateng either side of half-time. United levelled through a Ronaldo penalty controversially awarded for handball against Boateng. It was the last game for Larsson as his loan spell ended while Rooney, quiet of late, re-discovered his goal touch.

GEORGE BOATENG: "I'm devastated. It's a natural instinct when a shot is coming in to put your hands up to protect your face, that's all I did. It was a bad decision by the referee. We were the better team and should have won and we will be written off going to Old Trafford. But we'll give them a game in the replay."

GARETH SOUTHGATE: "We don't like to complain about referees but George is a yard away when it is flicked so I'm not sure what he could do to adjust his position."

SIR ALEX FERGUSON: "We never gave in and got our deserved equaliser. We'll now use our squad in the right way. We'll start utilising the pool."

MICHAEL CARRICK: "They had the momentum to come back and make it really hard. But the spirit here is unbelievable. You don't become a great team by playing pretty football and winning well every week. You have to grind out results and show character."

HENRIK LARSSON: "This is it. I am not 25 any more; I am 36 this year so it is not going to happen. I had a chat with Sir Alex but nothing would tempt me to change my mind... I know it is not good timing for me to leave now but that was the time period of the contract. I am confident they have enough to cope."

SIR ALEX FERGUSON: "Helsingborgs have their priorities and Henrik has promised that to them. He's got his family, too, there's no point in going on about it. I've spoken to the man and he's going back."

MIDDLESBROUGH		MANCHESTER UNITED	
Schwarzer		Kuszczak	
Parnaby		Neville	
Woodgate		Ferdinand	
Pogatetz		Vidic	
Taylor		Heinze	
Cattermole	⚽	Ronaldo	⚽
Subbed 80 mins (Morrison)		O'Shea	
Boateng	⚽	Carrick	
Subbed 89 mins (Euell)		Giggs	
Arca		Rooney	⚽
Downing		Larsson	
Yakuba		*Subs not used: Brown, Park, Smith, Richardson, Eagles*	
Viduka		**Coach: Sir Alex Ferguson**	
Subbed 89 mins (Lee)			
sub: Morrison			
sub: Euell			
Subs not used: Jones, Xavier			
Coach: Gareth Southgate			

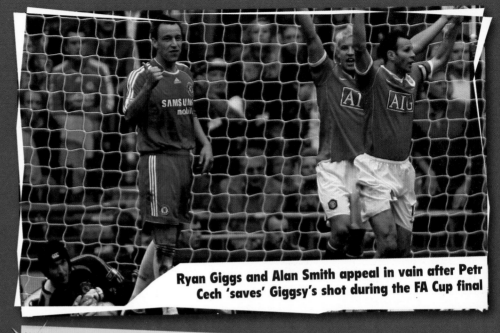

Ryan Giggs and Alan Smith appeal in vain after Petr Cech 'saves' Giggsy's shot during the FA Cup final

44

MANCHESTER UNITED 1
MIDDLESBROUGH 0

FA CUP QUARTER-FINAL REPLAY

DATE: Monday March 19

ATTENDANCE: 61,325 (Old Trafford)

REFEREE: Mike Dean

GOAL: 76 MINS (1-0) RONALDO - penalty. Ronaldo sent the goalkeeper the wrong way from the spot with a shot to the top-right corner – after Jonathan Woodgate had tripped him in the penalty area.

THE GAME: In the end not a great cup-tie. The best chance of the first-half arrived in the 42nd minute when Giggs threaded the ball through to Rooney. Rooney raced clear and went to round goalkeeper Schwarzer but the Middlesbrough man successfully dived and collected at Rooney's feet. On the hour Ronaldo hit the outside of a post while Rooney provoked a rare save from Schwarzer with a 23-yard shot. The tie was inevitably decided by a penalty, converted by Ronaldo, but conceded by Woodgate for a trip on the United player for which he was also booked.

RONALDO: "For me it was a penalty… of course I felt contact, that is why I slipped. If he touches me I lose my movement and that is why I go down. He kicked me. Maybe some people don't like me. Maybe I'm too good."

MANCHESTER UNITED	MIDDLESBROUGH
Kuszczak	Schwarzer
Brown	Xavier
Ferdinand	Woodgate
Vidic	Pogatetz
Heinze	Taylor
Ronaldo ⚽	*Subbed 89 mins (Huth)*
Carrick	Cattermole
Giggs	*Subbed 62 mins (Morrison)*
Richardson	Boateng
Subbed 61 mins (Park)	Arca
Rooney	*Subbed 69 mins (Rochemback)*
Smith	Downing
Subbed 71 mins (O'Shea)	Viduka
sub: Park	Yakubu
sub: O'Shea	*sub: Huth*
	sub: Morrison
Subs not used: *Cathcart, Eagles, Heaton*	*sub: Rochemback*
Coach: *Sir Alex Ferguson*	**Subs not used:** *Lee, Jones*
	Coach: *Gareth Southgate*

46

MANCHESTER UNITED 0
CHELSEA 1

FA CUP FINAL

DATE: Saturday May 19

ATTENDANCE: 89,826 (Wembley Stadium)

REFEREE: Steve Bennett

GOALS: 116 MINS (0-1) DROGBA - the big striker and Lampard performed a mid-air one-two on the edge of the area. Didier, with Van der Sar coming towards him and Ferdinand closing in behind, got the touch that propelled ball into the net.

THE GAME: The FA Cup final returned to the new Wembley Stadium with the top two teams in the land contesting a showpiece finale… except it was a terrible game! The match painfully went to extra-time and was decided by Drogba's 33rd goal of the season in the 116th minute. United may feel aggrieved that they had a perfectly good goal disallowed in the first period of extra-time when Rooney sent a superb cross in front of goal. Giggs slid in, Cech pounced, and the two players made contact. It appeared Cech had carried the ball over the goal-line with his momentum, but referee Bennett let play continue.

RYAN GIGGS: "It was clearly over the line – that was what I was asking for really. I've seen it over the line and he [referee Bennett] didn't give a free kick so it was a goal."

SIR ALEX FERGUSON: "There was nothing between the two teams, neither deserved to win and it is disappointing we have lost. The pitch was slow but I think we were tired in two or three positions."

MANCHESTER UNITED	CHELSEA
Van der Sar	Cech
Brown	Ferreira
Vidic	Essien
Ferdinand	Terry
Heinz	Bridge
Fletcher	Mikel
Subbed 92 mins (Smith)	Makelele
Scholes	Lampard
Carrick	Wright-Phillips
Subbed 112 mins (O'Shea)	*Subbed 83 mins (Kalou)*
Ronaldo	J Cole
Giggs	*Subbed HT (Robben (Cole 108))*
Subbed 112 mins (Solskjaer)	Drogba
Rooney	*sub: Kalou*
sub: Smith	*sub: Robben*
sub: O'Shea	**Subs not used:** *Cudicini, Diarra*
sub: Solskjaer	**Coach:** *Jose Mourinho*
Subs not used: *Kuszczak, Evra*	
Coach: *Sir Alex Ferguson*	

45

MANCHESTER UNITED 4
WATFORD 1

FA CUP SEMI-FINAL

DATE: Saturday April 14

ATTENDANCE: 37,425 (Villa Park)

REFEREE: Howard Webb

GOALS: 7 MINS (1-0) ROONEY - on the left, he received a pass from Carrick before he cut inside Adrian Mariappa and fired a right-foot shot from the edge of the area into the roof of the net; **26 MINS (1-1) BOUAZZA** - scored with an acrobatic left-foot volley that gave Van der Sar no chance; **28 MINS (2-1) RONALDO** - scored with a close-range tap-in after Rooney raced clear down the right and his cross-shot was deflected off Lee; **66 MINS (3-1) ROONEY** - side-footed home a Smith right-wing centre; **82 MINS (4-1) RICHARDSON** - was sent clear by Smith's through ball and Richardson finished off with a left foot shot into the far corner of the net.

THE GAME: Rooney was voted Player of the Round for his brilliant two-goal performance that saw United comfortably win through to the FA Cup final at the new Wembley Stadium.

United were hot favourites against the Premiership's bottom club and they did not fall short of their billing. An early lead through Rooney gave United the ideal start but Watford did not succumb and briefly got back on level terms through top scorer Hameur Bouazza until Ronaldo reinstated the lead. From that moment on, despite the loss of Ferdinand through injury, Manchester United and Rooney were in control and the outcome was never in doubt.

SIR ALEX FERGUSON: "The quality of our game when we got possession was fantastic. Rooney was out of this world… We're at the bare bones, but when you see the courage like Heinze and Brown exhibited today, you think you'll be okay. Watford have players who ask questions of you and Heinze and Brown had the courage to keep putting their heads in for the high balls."

RYAN GIGGS (IN MATCH PROGRAMME): "There are some players who have a fire within them and he is one of them. It's in his make-up. But take it out of him and you won't get the same effect as a player. It's all about striking a balance between that temperament and his ability… you just hope that the character of the player and the experiences of playing create that balance."

MANCHESTER UNITED	WATFORD
Van der Sar	Lee
Evra	Mariappa
Ferdinand	*Subbed 88 mins (Doyley)*
Subbed 40 mins (Fletcher)	Demerit
Brown	Carlisle
Heinze	Stewart
Ronaldo ⚽	Chambers
Subbed 77 mins (Richardson)	*Subbed 70 mins (Kabba)*
Scholes	Francis
Carrick	Mahon
Giggs	Smith
Subbed 83 mins (Solskjaer)	Priskin
Rooney ⚽⚽	*Subbed 78 mins (King)*
Smith	Bouazza ⚽
sub: Fletcher	*sub: Doyley*
sub: Richardson ⚽	*sub: Kabba*
sub: Solskjaer	*sub: King*
Subs not used: *Kuszczak, Cathcart*	**Subs not used:** *Loach, Bangura*
Coach: *Sir Alex Ferguson*	**Coach:** *Adrian Boothroyd*

CARLING CUP

MANCHESTER UNITED IN THE CARLING CUP

THE GAME: A potentially embarrassing night was narrowly averted by Kieran Lee's late, extra-time goal. In truth, League One side Crewe outplayed United for long periods and only the astute goalkeeping of Kuszczak kept Crewe from finding the net in the first-half. Indeed, Solskjaer's opening goal was very much against the run of play. Later, Richardson went close with two efforts for United which hit the crossbar and the foot of the post respectively.

SIR ALEX FERGUSON: "I am really disappointed with the performance. I told the players, 'These teams battle and make it hard, we have to match that', and we didn't do it. We allowed them to make the play... Crewe were very unlucky. They were the better team."

47
CREWE ALEXANDRA 1
MANCHESTER UNITED 2
AFTER EXTR-TIME

CARLING CUP THIRD ROUND

DATE: Wednesday October 25

ATTENDANCE: 10,046 (Alexandra Stadium)

REFEREE: Chris Foy

GOALS: 26 MINS (0-1) SOLSKJAER - Richard Jones got down the right and crossed to the near post for Solskjaer to shoot home from 12 yards; **73 MINS (1-1) VARNEY** - Luke Varney ran directly at the United defence, turned Brown and fired a low shot past Kuszczak into the far corner of the net; **119 MINS (1-2) LEE** - Kieran Lee fired home a powerful right-foot shot past goalkeeper Ben Williams.

CREWE ALEXANDRA	MANCHESTER UNITED
Williams	Kuszczak
Otsemobor	Gray
Baudet	*Subbed 77 mins (Lee)*
Subbed 110 mins (O'Donnell)	Brown
Cox	Silvestre
Taylor	Heinze
Subbed 76 mins (Bell)	Marsh
Lowe	*Subbed HT (Barnes) - subbed 103 mins (Shawcross)*
Rix	D Jones
Osbourne	R Jones
Vaughan	Richardson
Varney ⚽	Smith
Maynard	Solskjaer ⚽
sub: O'Donnell	*sub: Lee* ⚽
sub: Bell	*sub: Barnes*
	sub: Shawcross
Subs not used: Tomlinson, Rodgers, Higdon	**Subs not used:** Heaton, Rose
Coach: Dario Gradi	**Coach:** Sir Alex Ferguson

48
SOUTHEND UNITED 1
MANCHESTER UNITED 0

CARLING CUP FOURTH ROUND

DATE: Wednesday November 8

ATTENDANCE: 11,532 (Roots Hall)

REFEREE: Uriah Rennie

GOALS: 27 MINS (1-0) EASTWOOD - Shrimpers top scorer Freddy beat goalkeeper Kuszczak with a stunning 25-yard free kick after David Jones had fouled winger Jamal Campbell-Ryce.

THE GAME: Championship bottom of the table side Southend United caused a Carling Cup upset by beating a Manchester United side featuring Rooney and Ronaldo. Southend had won only two of their previous 16 matches but kept United at bay thanks to goalkeeper Darryl Flahavan who, among his stops, denied Ronaldo with two outstanding saves and had luck on his side when Jones hit the post shortly after Southend had taken the lead through Freddy Eastwood.

SIR ALEX FERGUSON: "It was a fantastic strike. I bet he doesn't score another goal like that in his life."

SOUTHEND	MANCHESTER UNITED
Flahavan	Kuszczak
Hunt	O'Shea
Subbed 13 mins (Francis)	*Subbed 75 mins (Lee)*
Sodje	Brown
Prior	Silvestre
Hammell	Heinze
Campbell-Ryce	Ronaldo
Clark	D Jones
Mayer	*Subbed 89 mins (Shawcross)*
Gower	Fletcher
Eastwood ⚽	Richardson
Hooper	Smith
Subbed 68 mins (Lawson)	*Subbed 60 mins (Evra)*
sub: Francis	Rooney
sub: Lawson	*sub: Lee*
Subs not used: Wilson, Cole, Moussa	*sub: Shawcross*
Coach: Steve Tilson	*sub: Evra*
	Subs not used: Heaton, Rose
	Coach: Sir Alex Ferguson

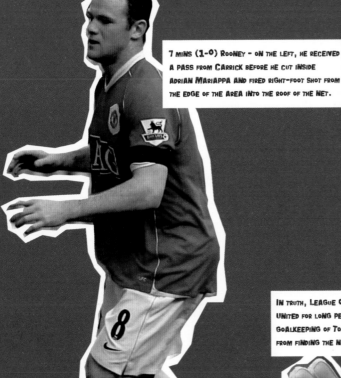

7 MINS (1-0) ROONEY - ON THE LEFT, HE RECEIVED A PASS FROM CARRICK BEFORE HE CUT INSIDE ADRIAN MARIAPPA AND FIRED RIGHT-FOOT SHOT FROM THE EDGE OF THE AREA INTO THE ROOF OF THE NET.

IN TRUTH, LEAGUE ONE SIDE CREWE OUTPLAYED UNITED FOR LONG PERIODS AND ONLY THE ASTUTE GOALKEEPING OF TOMASZ KUSZCZAK KEPT CREWE FROM FINDING THE NET IN THE FIRST-HALF.

UEFA CHAMPIONS LEAGUE

MANCHESTER UNITED IN THE CHAMPIONS LEAGUE

49

MANCHESTER UNITED 3
CELTIC 2

CHAMPIONS LEAGUE GROUP F

DATE: Wednesday September 13

ATTENDANCE: 74,031 (Old Trafford)

REFEREE: Lubos Michel (Slovakia)

GOALS: 21 MINS (0-1) VENNEGOOR OF HESSELINK - Jan Vennegoor, beating Ferdinand, was quickest to react and latched on to Artur Boruc's drop kick before driving a left foot shot past Van der Sar; **30 MINS (1-1) SAHA** - penalty. Saha fired low to the left to score from the spot after Boruc was adjudged to have brought down Giggs; **40 MINS (2-1) SAHA** - hit a first-time shot through the goalkeeper's legs and into the net from a Scholes pass; **43 MINS (2-2) NAKAMURA** - the Japanese midfielder curled a left-foot free kick into the top right-hand corner of the net from 25 yards out; **47 MINS (3-2) SOLSKJAER** - Scholes intercepted a Thomas Gravesen pass in midfield and found Saha on the edge of the area. Saha's shot was saved by Boruc and his followed up attempt went sideways allowing Solskjaer to side foot home.

THE GAME: An exciting all-British encounter and the first competitive meeting between Manchester United and Glasgow Celtic. The game marked the return to the United side since his suspension for Rooney and Scholes. Four goals were shared in the first-half where both teams led at different times. The match winner came shortly after the break but there could have been more goals but for excellent goalkeeping work by Van der Sar – in particular for denying Gravesen late on – and Boruc – for saving shots from Saha, Rooney and a header from his own player, midfielder Paul Telfer.

SIR ALEX FERGUSON: "Celtic had a go all night which is typical of the history of that club. But in fairness to our lads, some of our attacking play was really good and we could have had more goals. We could have scored ten to be honest with you."

LOUIS SAHA: "It was one of those games where you get so many opportunities but two goals is not so bad."

MANCHESTER UNITED	CELTIC
Van der Sar	Boruc
Neville	Wilson
Ferdinand	Subbed 52 mins (Telfer)
Brown	Caldwell
Silvestre	McManus
Fletcher	Naylor
Scholes	Lennon
Subbed 80 mins (O'Shea)	Nakamura
Carrick	Gravesen
Giggs	Jarosik
Subbed 33 mins (Solskjaer)	Subbed 56 mins (Miller)
Rooney	McGeady
Subbed 86 mins (Richardson)	Subbed 70 mins (Maloney)
Saha	Vennegoor of Hesselink
sub: O'Shea	sub: Telfer
sub: Solskjaer	sub: Miller
sub: Richardson	sub: Maloney
Subs not used: Kuszczak, Evra, Smith, Vidic	Subs not used: Marshall, Balde, Zurawski, Sno
Coach: Sir Alex Ferguson	Coach: Gordon Strachan

50

BENFICA 0
MANCHESTER UNITED 1

CHAMPIONS LEAGUE GROUP F

DATE: Tuesday September 26

ATTENDANCE: 61,000 (Estadio da Luz)

REFEREE: Frank De Bleeckere (Belgium)

GOAL: 60 MINS (1-0) SAHA - received a Ronaldo pass before cutting inside from the right and unleashing a powerful left foot shot that took a slight deflection off Anderson, past keeper Quim, and into the net.

THE GAME: Manchester United secured a hard-earned win at the Estadio da Luz. They were fortunate in that Benfica, for all their play helped in no small way by United giving away possession, lacked penetration. United were solid at the back and played Saha as a lone striker with Rooney out on the left of a five-man midfield. Chances were few and far between before the goal and then Benfica were forced to open up more. Goalkeeper Quim was provoked into making successive saves from Heinze's free kick and the follow-up efforts of Fletcher and Carrick.

SIR ALEX FERGUSON: "We were scratching through the first-half, giving the ball away in defensive positions. Unlike last time we were prepared to defend properly."

BENFICA	MANCHESTER UNITED
Quim	Van der Sar
Alcides	Neville
Luisao	Ferdinand
Anderson	Vidic
Subbed 82 mins (Mantorras)	Heinze
Leo	Ronaldo
Petit	Carrick
Katsouranis	O'Shea
Karagounis	Scholes
Subbed 62 mins (Nuno Assis)	Rooney
Paulo Jorge	Subbed 85 mins (Fletcher)
Subbed 65 mins (Miccoli)	Saha
Nuno Gomes	Subbed 85 mins (Smith)
Simao	sub: Fletcher
sub: Mantorras	sub: Smith
sub: Nuno Assis	Subs not used: Kuszczak, Evra, Brown, Solskjaer, Richardson
sub: Miccoli	
Subs not used: Moretto, Beto, Nelson, Ricardo Rocha	Coach: Sir Alex Ferguson
Coach: Fernando Santos	

51

MANCHESTER UNITED 3
FC COPENHAGEN 0

CHAMPIONS LEAGUE GROUP F

DATE: Tuesday October 17

ATTENDANCE: 72,020 (Old Trafford)

REFEREE: Frank Jan Wegereef (Holland)

GOALS: 39 MINS (1-0) SCHOLES - Evra attacked down the left who passed to Saha. He set up Scholes to score a sensational goal with a long-range shot into the corner of the net; **46 MINS (2-0) O'SHEA** - Ronaldo's corner saw O'Shea instinctively flick the ball goalward but it struck his standing foot and heel before going into the net; **83 MINS (3-0) RICHARDSON** - fired in an innocuous shot that somehow squeezed past goalkeeper Jesper Christiansen as he slipped.

THE GAME: A week before his 21st birthday, Rooney skippered Manchester United to a comprehensive 3-0 victory over Danish champions FC Copenhagen. Rooney led the side out after the late withdrawals of Ferdinand, with a cricked neck, and Giggs, who complained of feeling unwell in the dressing room and asked to be put on the bench. Brown and Fletcher were also drafted into the side as a result. The Rooney-led United were unstoppable as the Danes were put under unremitting pressure that was converted into goals by Scholes, O'Shea and Richardson. Rooney, himself, carved out several chances for Saha and Solskjaer and also went close himself with a lob that beat the goalkeeper and had Danish defender Michael Gravgaard racing back to clear the unprotected goal.

WAYNE ROONEY: "I was pleased to get the armband, but it wasn't the main issue of the night. We're really pleased, we got three goals and three points and it an important win. We had a lot of chances but at the end of the day we're just happy to get three points."

SIR ALEX FERGUSON: "Some players, like Paul Scholes, don't want to be captain, so it was an easy choice and Wayne did fantastically, as I expected."

MANCHESTER UNITED	FC COPENHAGEN
Van der Sar	Christiansen
O'Shea	Jacobsen
Brown	Hangeland
Vidic	Gravgaard
Evra	Wendt
Ronaldo	Linedroth
Carrick	Silberhauer
Subbed 60 mins (Solskjaer)	Subbed 82 mins (Bergvold)
Scholes	Norregaard
Subbed 76 mins (Richardson)	Subbed 57 mins (Kvist)
Fletcher	Hutchinson
Saha	Berglund
Subbed 60 mins (Smith)	Subbed 57 mins (Pimpong)
Rooney	Allback
sub: Solskjaer	sub: Bervold
sub: Richardson	sub: Kvist
sub: Smith	sub: Pimpong
Subs not used: Kuszczak, Giggs, D Jones	Subs not used: Gall, Thomasson, Brandrupo, Hansen
Coach: Sir Alex Ferguson	Coach: Stale Solbakken

> **"DURING THE WARM-UP RIO MANAGED TO INJURE HIMSELF. WITH GARY NEVILLE ALREADY OUT WITH INJURY AND GIGGSY NOT FEELING WELL AT ALL, I WAS MADE-UP, DEAD PLEASED TO BE HANDED THE CAPTAIN'S ARMBAND BY ALBERT OUR KIT MAN"**

52 — FC COPENHAGEN 1 / MANCHESTER UNITED 0

CHAMPIONS LEAGUE GROUP F

DATE: Wednesday November 1

ATTENDANCE: 40,000 (Parken Stadium)

REFEREE: Wolfgang Stark (Germany)

GOAL: 73 MINS (1-0) ALLBACK - Heinze failed to head clear a left-wing cross, Atiba Hutchinson headed down for Marcus Allback, in a crowded penalty area, who managed to shoot home from inside six-yard box.

THE GAME: Manchester United, with six changes from the side that beat Bolton 4-0, gave a sub-standard performance in sub-zero temperatures as they suffered a shock 1-0 defeat by the Danish champions. The pitch was muddy and rutted as a result of a rock concert the previous weekend and the unwelcoming weather conditions of downpour and the occasional blizzard did not help. Chances were few and far between as Rooney and Ronaldo could not make an impact and save for Allback's match-winning goal, Van der Sar was untroubled. Ronaldo did have the ball in the net from a Rooney cross in stoppage time, but the effort was ruled out because of offside.

SIR ALEX FERGUSON: "The pitch was very difficult and that's why it was the game it was. There wasn't a lot of football. It wasn't an easy pitch and it took us 20 minutes just to get any rhythm."

FC COPENHAGEN	MANCHESTER UNITED
Christiansen	Van der Sar
Jacobsen	Brown
Hangeland	Vidic
Gravgaard	Subbed HT (Ferdinand)
Wendt	Silvestre
Silberhauer	Heinze
Subbed 71 mins (Kvist)	Subbed 80 mins (Evra)
Linderoth	Fletcher
Norregaard	Subbed 71 mins (Scholes)
Bergvold	Carrick
Subbed 68 mins (Berglund)	O'Shea
Allback ⚽	Ronaldo
Subbed 89 mins (Thomassen)	Rooney
Hutchinson	Solskjaer
sub: Kvist	sub: Ferdinand
sub: Berglund	sub: Evra
sub: Thomassen	sub: Scholes
Subs not used: Gall, Pimpong	Subs not used: Kuszczak,
Coach: Stale Solbakken	Smith, Richardson, D Jones
	Coach: Sir Alex Ferguson

53 — CELTIC 1 / MANCHESTER UNITED 0

CHAMPIONS LEAGUE GROUP F

DATE: Tuesday November 21

ATTENDANCE: 60,632 (Celtic Park)

REFEREE: Mejuto Gonzalez (Spain)

GOAL: 81 MINS (1-0) NAKAMURA - as at Old Trafford, Nakamura scored direct from a free-kick with a left-foot curling shot into the top right hand corner after Vidic had fouled Jari Jarosik.

THE GAME: Saha had an 88th minute penalty saved by goalkeeper Artur Boruc after Neil Lennon was penalised and booked for handball. It summed up the Frenchman's night. Moments earlier he had been put clear inside the area by a Rooney chipped pass. He was in an offside position, realised it and finished off with a casual shot. Unfortunately, there was no flag or whistle from the match officials and the incident went down as a missed chance. United made few chances on the night and the result meant Celtic qualified for the last 16 for the time while United's place was put on hold for the time being.

SIR ALEX FERGUSON: "We're disappointed. We threw it away, no question. We had some good opportunities but our finishing was disappointing."

CELTIC	MANCHESTER UNITED
Boruc	Van der Sar
Telfer	Neville
Balde	Ferdinand
McManus	Vidic
Naylor	Heinze
Nakamura ⚽	Subbed 87 mins (Evra)
Subbed 85 mins (Miller)	Ronaldo
Gravesen	Carrick
Lennon	Subbed 87 mins (O'Shea)
Sno	Scholes
Subbed HT (Jarosik)	Giggs
Vennegoor of Hesselink	Saha
Zurawski	Rooney
Subbed HT (Maloney)	sub: Evra
sub: Miller	sub: O'Shea
sub: Jarosik	Coach: Sir Alex Ferguson
sub: Maloney	Subs not used: Kuszczak,
Coach: Gordon Strachan	Brown, Richardson, Fletcher,
Subs not used: Marshall,	Silvestre
Wilson, McGeady, O'Dea	

54 — MANCHESTER UNITED 3 / BENFICA 1

CHAMPIONS LEAGUE GROUP F

DATE: Wednesday December 6

ATTENDANCE: 74,955 (Old Trafford)

REFEREE: Herbert Fandel (Germany)

GOALS: 27 MINS (0-1) NELSON - a superb run by Simao ended with him reaching byline to pull the ball back into space on to which the forward-charging Nelson unleashed a powerful 30-yard angled shot into the top right-hand corner of the net; 45 MINS (1-1) VIDIC - Giggs' free-kick into the area was met by the charging Vidic to score with a glancing header past Quim; 61 MINS (2-1) GIGGS - unmarked, he jumped to head Ronaldo's cross purposefully into the net past Quim; 75 MINS (3-1) SAHA - Fletcher's corner was headed home by Saha.

THE GAME: All United had to do to qualify was to avoid defeat against the Portuguese side that knocked them out of the Champions League the previous season. When Nelson gave Benfica a 27th minute lead the alarm bells of disappointment were ringing in the United's faithful's ears. However, recovery, victory and, ultimately, winning through to the last 16 as Group F winners was to emerge thanks to three headed goals from Vidic, Giggs and Saha. Vidic's goal was the most significant on the stroke of half-time. That equaliser provided inspiration for the home side and a disheartening trepidation for the visitors that 45 minutes later left United victorious and Benfica seeking solace in the UEFA Cup.

SIR ALEX FERGUSON: "When Benfica scored, that was what lifted us. As the game went on we got better and better. We got good penetration, put Rooney back up front in his normal position, and that made a difference."

MANCHESTER UNITED	BENFICA
Van der Sar	Quim
Neville	Nelson ⚽
Ferdinand	Luisao
Vidic ⚽	Ricardo Rocha
Evra	Lito
Subbed 67 mins (Heinze)	Katsouranis
Ronaldo	Petit
Carrick	Simao
Scholes	Nuno Assis
Subbed 79 mins (Solskjaer)	Subbed 73 mins (Karagounis)
Giggs ⚽	Nuno Gomes
Subbed 74 mins (Fletcher)	Miccoli
Saha ⚽	Subbed 64 mins (Paulo Jorge)
Rooney	sub: Karagounis
sub: Heinze	sub: Paulo Jorge
sub: Solskjaer	Subs not used: Moretto,
sub: Fletcher	Anderson, Mantorras,
Subs not used: Kuszczak,	Miguelito, Beto
Brown, O'Shea, Silvestre	Coach: Fernando Santos
Coach: Sir Alex Ferguson	

55 — LILLE 0 / MANCHESTER UNITED 1

CHAMPIONS LEAGUE

LAST 16, FIRST LEG

DATE: Tuesday February 20

ATTENDANCE: 41,000 (Stade Felix-Bollaert, Lens)

REFEREE: Eric Braamhaar (Holland)

GOAL: 83 MINS (0-1) GIGGS - hit a superb quickly-taken free kick into the top corner of the net while Lille were still sorting out their defence.

THE GAME: This was a terrible game to watch which was ultimately decided in controversial fashion. Giggs scored his 25th goal in club competition with a quickly-taken free kick. The Lille players were furious as they were still sorting out their defensive wall but Dutch referee Eric Braamhaar said that the goal would stand. The Lille officials were so enraged they tried to pull the team off the pitch but were eventually persuaded to complete the game. There was further grief for the fans, some of whom were injured, as a terrifying crush was created down to poor stadium organisation.

SIR ALEX FERGUSON: "I've never seen anything like it. They were trying to intimidate the referee, incite the fans and create a hostile atmosphere. It is an absolute disgrace what happened tonight."

LILLE	MANCHESTER UNITED
Sylva	Van der Sar
Chalme	Neville
Plestan	Vidic
Tavlaridis	Ferdinand
Tafforeau	Evra
Debuchy	Carrick
Bodmer	Scholes
Obraniak	Subbed 90 mins (O'Shea)
Subbed 89 mins (Bastos)	Ronaldo
Makoun	Subbed 66 mins (Saha)
Fanvergue	Giggs ⚽
Subbed 57 mins (Cabaye)	Larsson
Odemwingie	Rooney
Subbed 75 mins (Audel)	sub: O'Shea
sub: Bastos	sub: Saha
sub: Cabaye	Subs not used: Kuszczak,
sub: Audel	Brown, Park, Fletcher, Silvestre
Subs not used: Malicki, Rafael,	Coach: Sir Alex Ferguson
Lichtsteiner, Mirallas	
Coach: Claude Puel	

"I WAS WALKING BACK AS IF TO TAKE THE FREE-KICK, LINING MYSELF UP, WHEN I HEARD RYAN SHOUT AT ME, 'PUT IT DOWN, I'LL TAKE IT'. HE SENT IT ARROWING INTO THE NET BEFORE THE GOALIE COULD MOVE OR THE WALL COULD DO ANYTHING. GIGGSY TOLD ME AFTERWARDS THAT THE REF HAD ASKED HIM IF HE WANTED A WHISTLE — AND HE'D SAID NO. THE LILLE PLAYERS WERE FURIOUS OF COURSE. THEY RAN OFF THE PITCH. I THOUGHT THEY WERE REFUSING TO PLAY ON, BUT APPARENTLY THEY WERE JUST GOING TO TALK TO THEIR COACH ABOUT WHAT TO DO NEXT. APPARENTLY THAT HAPPENS IN FRANCE. I'D NEVER SEEN ANYTHING LIKE IT BEFORE, THE OTHER TEAM LEAVING THE PITCH"

56

MANCHESTER UNITED 1
LILLE 0

CHAMPIONS LEAGUE

LAST 16, SECOND LEG

DATE: Wednesday March 7

ATTENDANCE: 75,182 (Old Trafford)

REFEREE: Luis Medina Cantalejo (Spain)

GOAL: 72 MINS (1-0) LARSSON - headed home Ronaldo's cross from the byline.

THE GAME: It was a forgettable return leg against Lille and any ill-feeling from the first leg was not obviously apparent. Both sides did hit the woodwork with O'Shea heading against the crossbar and Osaze Odemwingie hitting the post. The game was decided by a piece of Ronaldo skill, who set up Larsson with a header to put the score 2-0 on aggregate and beyond Lille's reach. The result sent Manchester United through to the Champions League quarter-finals for the first time in four years.

MANCHESTER UNITED	LILLE	
Van der Sar	Sylva	
Neville	Chalme	
Vidic	Plestan	
Ferdinand	Tavlaridis	
Silvestre	Tafforeau	
Carrick	Bastos	
Scholes	*Subbed HT (Debuchy)*	
Ronaldo	Keita	
Subbed 82 mins (Richardson)	Obraniak	
Giggs	Makoun	
Rooney	Dumont	
Subbed 82 mins (Park)	*Subbed 74 mins (Fanvergue)*	
Larsson ⚽	Odemwingie	
Subbed 74 mins (Smith)	*Subbed 74 mins (Mirallas)*	
sub: Richardson	*sub: Debuchy*	
sub: Park	*sub: Fanvergue*	
sub: Smith	*sub: Mirallas*	
Subs not used: Kuszczak, Heinze, Brown, Giggs	*Subs not used: Malicki, Rafael, Lichtsteiner, Mirallas*	
Coach: Sir Alex Ferguson	*Coach: Claude Puel*	

"WE COULD SEE THE ROMA PLAYERS WERE IN SHOCK AND WANTED IT ALL OVER! IT FINISHED 7-1 AND I CAN SAY THAT ALL THE GOALS, THEIRS INCLUDED, WERE EXCELLENT. FROM PROPER MOVES, BITS OF INDIVIDUAL SKILL, NONE OF THEM WERE JAMMY OR SCRAMBLED OR DEFLECTED. WE WERE INTO THE SEMI-FINALS ALONG WITH TWO OTHER ENGLISH SIDES!"

57

ROMA 2
MANCHESTER UNITED 1

CHAMPIONS LEAGUE

QUARTER-FINAL, FIRST LEG

DATE: Wednesday April 4

ATTENDANCE: 75,000 (Stadio Olimpico)

REFEREE: Herbert Fandel

GOALS: 44 MINS (1-0) TADDEI - Midfielder Rodrigo Taddei fired a left-foot shot from 12 yards out that deflected off Brown and into the net after receiving a pull back from Mancini; **60 MINS (1-1) ROONEY** - the move was carried forward by the pace and skill of Ronaldo. Then Solskjaer's first-time, far-post cross was chested down and then fired into back of the net by Rooney; **66 MINS (2-1) VUCINEC** - Mancini's right-foot rising shot from 30 yards produced a quick reaction parried save from Van der Sar but Mirko Vucinec slided in to score with the rebound.

THE GAME: Manchester United suffered their first defeat in 15 games but stayed in the tie thanks to Rooney's all-important away goal. It was his first European goal in two-and-a-half years and United's 100th goal of 2006-07 season. Rooney had been cast in the part of support forward, rotating position with Ronaldo, and spending much of tie in wide areas. It was a role that gained greater significance following the 34th minute dismissal of Scholes. He had committed four fouls by the 26th minute for his first caution and a further bookable foul on Francesco Totti eight minutes later led to his sending off. Sadly, the half-time break was tarnished by the over-reaction of the Italian police towards the United fans following the Roma opening goal.

WAYNE ROONEY: "We were both young and trying to learn the game when we played against an Italian defence two years ago. Playing against the likes of Maldini and Nesta gave us a good platform to learn. From there, me and Cristiano have improved as players, we have matured a lot, especially Cristiano, who has been winning games on his own this season. He has been unbelievable – at the minute he is by far the best player in the world."

SIR ALEX FERGUSON: "It is a question of interpretation with Paul. How you can tackle in England is not how you can tackle in Italy or Germany. There is a lack of understanding and knowledge of British players and Paul is suffering because of that. He should not have got sent off for the second booking. The lad went charging towards the referee. Then, after he had sent Paul off, he clapped him and patted him on the back. That is unacceptable. Roma as a club I have no problem with but Chivu is a different breed."

ROMA	MANCHESTER UNITED	
Doni	Van der Sar	
Cassetti	Brown	
Mexes	O'Shea	
Chivu	Ferdinand	
Panucci	Heinze	
De Rossi	Ronaldo	
Wilhelmsson	Carrick	
Subbed 62 mins (Vucinec)	Scholes	
Taddei ⚽	Giggs	
Subbed 82 mins (Rosi)	*Subbed 77 mins (Saha)*	
Perrotta	Rooney	
Mancini	Solskjaer	
Totti	*Subbed 72 mins (Fletcher)*	
sub: Vucinec ⚽	*sub: Saha*	
sub: Rosi	*sub: Fletcher*	
Subs not used: Curci, Faty, Defendi, Ferrari, Okaka Chuka	*Subs not used: Kuszczak, Smith, Dong, Richardson, Eagles*	
Coach: Luciano Spalletti	*Coach: Sir Alex Ferguson*	

58

MANCHESTER UNITED 7
ROMA 1
MANCHESTER UNITED WON 8-3 ON AGGREGATE

CHAMPIONS LEAGUE

QUARTER-FINAL, SECOND LEG

DATE: Tuesday April 10

ATTENDANCE: 74,476 (Old Trafford)

REFEREE: Lubos Michel (Slovakia)

GOALS: 12 MINS (1-0) CARRICK - Ronaldo carried the ball forward from the half-way line before squaring it to Carrick who thumped a rising right-foot shot from 15 yards into the top of the net; **17 MINS (2-0) SMITH** - Heinze hit a first-time pass into Giggs from the left. Giggs turned, beat a defender, then laid the ball off to Smith to score with a right-foot shot from the edge of the area; **19 MINS (3-0) ROONEY** - Fletcher gained possession inside his own penalty area and instigated a pitch-length move involving O'Shea, then laid the ball off to Ronaldo – who beat two players – Smith and Giggs, who centred perfectly for Rooney to race in and side-foot home in off the base of the post; **44 MINS (4-0) RONALDO** - unmarked Ronaldo on the right flank halfway inside the Roma half received a long pass from Giggs, he advanced, cut inside and, despite the closing defenders, managed to fire home a right foot shot between goalkeeper Doni and the right post; **49 MINS (5-0) RONALDO** - slid in at the far post to score at close range from a Giggs left-wing cross; **60 MINS (6-0) CARRICK** - unleashed a powerful 25-yard right foot shot into the top right-hand corner of the net from Heinze's pass; **69 MINS (6-1) DE ROSSI** - netted with a superb 12-yard volley from Totti's right-wing cross; **81 MINS (7-1) EVRA** - United attacked down the left flank with Evra, Rooney and Solskjaer before Evra received the ball back on the edge of the area to strike a low left foot shot in off the right post.

THE GAME: Manchester United recorded their biggest win in Europe for 39 years as they progressed through to the European Champions League semi-finals for the first time in five years with an exhilarating display. United were at their breathtaking best quickly cancelling out the one goal deficit from the first leg and then went on a goal-fest that left Roma - no minnow remember - completely shell-shocked. The quality of the play and the quality of the goals were outstanding and there could have been other goals too.

RIO FERDINAND: "We were breathtaking. To do that after losing to Portsmouth showed great spirit and bouncebackability!"

PATRICE EVRA: "We don't spend much time having doubts here. That's the difference between a great club and an average club... I thought it was a joke by Ferguson when he sent me on at right-back. I scored by accident, really... we need to win something this year. If you win nothing people will say, 'Well, United played good football', but to me that is not enough. If we win nothing it will have been a bad season. We must win one trophy... we've been playing well all season. We are a team of great character."

EDWIN VAN DER SAR: "I have never seen a performance like that before in my career."

MICHAEL CARRICK: "I've been on the end of a few score lines like that in my youth team days at West Ham and to do it on a night of such importance, against a team with such a defensive record like Roma's, is just incredible."

RONALDO: "I'm pleased I've finally scored my first goals in the Champions League – I'm very happy."

MANCHESTER UNITED	ROMA	
Van der Sar	Doni	
O'Shea	Cassetti	
Subbed 52 mins (Evra)	Mexes	
Ferdinand	Chivu	
Brown	Panucci	
Heinze	De Rossi ⚽	
Fletcher	*Subbed 86 mins (Faty)*	
Carrick ⚽⚽	Pizarro	
Subbed 73 mins (Richardson)	Wilhelmsson	
Ronaldo ⚽⚽	*Subbed 88 mins (Rosi)*	
Giggs	Vucinic	
Subbed 61 mins (Solskjaer)	Mancini	
Rooney ⚽	*Subbed 90 mins (Okaka Chuka)*	
Smith ⚽	Totti	
sub: Evra ⚽	*sub: Faty*	
sub: Richardson	*sub: Rosi*	
sub: Solskjaer	*sub: Okaka Chuka*	
Subs not used: Kuszczak, Dong, Cathcart, Eagles	*Subs not used: Curci, Defendi, Ferrari*	
Coach: Sir Alex Ferguson	*Coach: Luciano Spalletti*	

59 MANCHESTER UNITED 3
AC MILAN 2

CHAMPIONS LEAGUE

SEMI-FINAL, FIRST LEG

DATE: Tuesday April 24

ATTENDANCE: 73,820 (Old Trafford)

REFEREE: Kyros Vassaras (Greece)

GOALS: 5 MINS (1-0) DIDA - OWN GOAL. Ronaldo's header, from a Giggs right-wing corner, hit Dida's arm and he got a desperate touch with his hand but the ball ended up in the net; 22 MINS (1-1) KAKA - the Brazilian received the ball from Clarence Seedorf then with guile and speed, beat three United defenders before slipping the ball past a static Van der Sar from close range; 37 MINS (1-2) KAKA - Kaka escaped Fletcher on the left with a header, Evra and Heinze collided with one another leaving Kaka with the gift of a right foot shot past Van der Sar from 12 yards; 59 MINS (2-2) ROONEY - a brilliant lofted pass from Scholes into the area for Rooney to fire low underneath the goalkeeper with a right foot shot; 90 MINS (3-2) ROONEY - fired home from the edge of the area with a right foot shot between goalkeeper and the right post after he received an excellent reverse pass from Giggs.

THE GAME: Rooney inspired Manchester United to a stunning comeback and ultimately a dramatic victory in a thrilling European tie against Italian giants AC Milan. Rooney's persistence, movement and energy caused all sorts of problems for experienced Milan central partnership of Paolo Maldini and Alessandro Nesta. The own goal gave United the ideal start but Milan responded and with the gifted Kaka exploiting any errors by the United defence, he scored twice to give the visitors the lead before the break. It took a piece of inspirational skill from Scholes and composed finishing from Rooney to level the scores. But with a draw looking on the cards, a stoppage time winner created by captain Giggs and scored by Rooney clinched victory – United's 99th victory in the European Cup – on another magical European night for the club.

WAYNE ROONEY: "It was a great feeling, a difficult match. We kept on going until the end. The goal in the last minute was a great feeling... I've seen him [Scholes] do that everyday in training. He's an absolute joy to play with. He's a genius."

KAKA: "Their whole team impressed me. Their system is set up to attack, to put pressure on the opposition and it's great to watch. We are two similar, well-matched teams who can both think about going through to the final."

SIR ALEX FERGUSON: "We persevered. We kept playing our football. I thought some of the football was fantastic. I think in the second-half we dominated it."

MANCHESTER UNITED	AC MILAN
Van der Sar	Dida
Evra	Oddo
Heinze	Nesta
Brown	Maldini
O'Shea	*Subbed HT (Bonera)*
Ronaldo	Jankulovski
Fletcher	Gattuso
Carrick	*Subbed 52 mins (Brocchi)*
Scholes	Pirlo
Giggs	Ambrosini
Rooney	Seedorf
	Kaka
	Gilardino
	Subbed 84 mins (Gourcuff)
Subs not used: Kuczszak, Smith, Solskjaer, Fangzhuo, Richardson, Eagles, Lee	*sub: Bonera*
Coach: Sir Alex Ferguson	*sub: Brocchi*
	sub: Gourcuff
	Subs not used: Kalac, Cafu, Inzaghi, Favalli
	Coach: Carlo Ancelotti

"THE RAIN WAS TORRENTIAL, WORSE THAN MANCHESTER, BUT THAT WAS NO EXCUSE FOR WHAT HAPPENED. WE WERE TWO-DOWN BEFORE WE REALISED WHAT HAD HAPPENED. AND THAT WAS IT REALLY. WE NEVER RECOVERED. CLARENCE SEEDORF WAS TERRIFIC - I NEVER REALISED HE WAS SO GOOD — AND KAKA WAS MASTERLY"

60 AC MILAN 3
MANCHESTER UNITED 0

AC MILAN WON 5-3 ON AGGREGATE

CHAMPIONS LEAGUE

SEMI-FINAL, SECOND LEG

DATE: Wednesday May 2

ATTENDANCE: 78,000 (San Siro Stadium)

REFEREE: Frank De Bleeckere (Belgium)

GOALS: 11 MINS (1-0) KAKA - Oddo long ball, flicked perfectly by Seedorf into path of Kaka, who fired a low shot past Van der Sar just inside the right post; 30 MINS (2-0) SEEDORF - Vidic slipped while undertaking an attempted clearance inside the United area from Heinze's pass. The ball was intercepted and brought under control by Andrea Pirlo on the right flank and he crossed from the byline. Vidic's header away went to Seedorf on the edge of the area and the Dutchman, despite Vidic's sliding tackle, hit a low volley into the net; 78 MINS (3-0) GILARDINO - Massimo Ambrosini set sub Alberto Gilardino clear and he poked the ball home past the advancing goalkeeper.

THE GAME: On a rain-soaked night in Milan, on the Italian side's brand new pitch, Manchester United gave the worst performance of their European season. Poor defending, coupled with ruthless exploitation of those errors by an excellent Milan side, saw United crash out by 3-0 - their worst defeat of the season. Dreams of another final were put on hold for another year.

SIR ALEX FERGUSON: "They were better prepared physically, they've been resting players and that can make a difference. They were certainly sharper and quicker and have been good winners."

AC MILAN	MANCHESTER UNITED
Dida	Van der Sar
Oddo	O'Shea
Nesta	*Subbed 77 mins (Saha)*
Kaladze	Brown
Jankulovski	Vidic
Gattuso	Heinze
Subbed 85 mins (Cafu)	Fletcher
Pirlo	Scholes
Ambrosini	Carrick
Seedorf	Ronaldo
Kaka	Rooney
Subbed 86 mins (Favalli)	Giggs
Inzaghi	*sub: Saha*
Subbed 67 mins (Gilardino)	
sub: Cafu	*Subs not used: Kuszczak, Ferdinand, Smith, Solskjaer, Richardson, Eagles*
sub: Favalli	*Coach: Sir Alex Ferguson*
sub: Gilardino	
Subs not used: Kalac, Bonera, Serginho, Brocchi	
Coach: Carlo Ancelotti	

Cristiano Ronaldo torments Massimo Oddo and Gennaro Gattuso during the Champions League semi-final, second leg